BASEBALL'S HALL OF FAME

JERRY BRONDFIELD

SCHOLASTIC INC.

New York Toronto London Auckland Sydney Tokyo

ISBN 0-590-32763-1

12 11 10 9 8 7 6 5 4 3 2   4 5 6 7 8/8

Printed in the U.S.A.   01

ALL-TIME SUPERSTARS

NEW
HALL-of-FAMERS

As we went to press, two players were elected to the Hall of Fame for 1983: Third baseman Brooks Robinson of the Baltimore Orioles, and pitcher Juan Marichal of the San Francisco Giants.

The National Baseball Hall of Fame and Museum at Cooperstown, New York.

INTRODUCTION

It seems as though every sport has its Hall of Fame: baseball, basketball, pro football, college football, swimming—just about everything but croquet—but probably the best and most colorful is Baseball's Hall of Fame at Cooperstown, N.Y.

It was opened in 1939 as the centerpiece of the game's 100th anniversary. Every year since then it has been a magnet for baseball fans who visit it from every state in the Union. Outside of, perhaps, the World Series, it is the finest show in baseball, and no kid (or his parents) should miss it if he's anywhere in the neighborhood.

1

The Ball Parks Room: mementos from around the major leagues.

Although there have been many theories how baseball came into existence, it has been generally agreed that it owes its most direct link to Abner Doubleday. Doubleday, a native of Cooperstown, was a schoolboy when he and his pals swatted around a crude, cloth-stuffed ball with a fat stick. Most evidence points to the fact that it was young Abner Doubleday who got the idea for a formal scheme of hitting the ball and running between designated points. He marked out a square-shaped plot with stations, or bases, at each corner, then turned it so that it looked like a diamond. He devised some crude rules for the hitting and running and scoring, and baseball was under way. Over the years there would be a lot of changes and refinements, of course. But it was Abner Doubleday's imagination and the respect his buddies had for him that made him the igniting spark of the sport.

Abner Doubleday went on to become a cadet at West Point. He served with honors in the Mexican War and in the Civil War. In fact, it was Captain Abner Doubleday who ordered the firing of the first Union shot in defense of Fort Sumter, S.C., in the battle that launched the Civil War. Few Americans have such diversified fame as Doubleday's invention of the nation's leading sport and helping start the nation's most dramatic military conflict.

In 1935, the presidents of the National and American Leagues and the commissioner of baseball began to consider the possibility of a shrine for baseball in time for the game's 100th anniversary. Some relics—

Courtesy of the Baseball Hall of Fame.

Memorabilia of great players and events in the game's history.

old balls and bats and photos of the game as played in the 1840s—had been on display in the town hall at Cooperstown. They were objects of great interest to hundreds of visitors from around upper New York State.

So, baseball's modern leaders figured if there was going to be a real museum it certainly belonged in Cooperstown, where it had all started. It would be called Baseball's Hall of Fame.

Four years later—in 1939—it opened to great acclaim, in a lovely, red brick building especially designed to hold the many great mementos of the sport. It would be a fitting shrine to the immortal stars who had shone in the past and those who would contribute so much in the future.

Then the questions came: How would these stars be chosen for the Hall, and who would elect them? It was decided that the electors would be members of the Baseball Writers of America who had been active writers for at least 10 years.

The electors would have certain rules to follow. Among them: In order for a player to be elected to the Hall, he had to have been active in the major leagues during a period beginning 20 years before his election year and ending at least five years before his election year. The player also must have played in each of at least 10 big league seasons.

In case of the death of an active player or one who has been retired less than five full years, a candidate who is otherwise eligible would become eligible in the next regular election held at least six months after his death, or after the end of the five-year period. If it sounds complicated, don't worry; the baseball writers who do the electing know what it's all about.

In brief, voting is based on the player's record, his playing ability, his sportsmanship, his character, and his contribution to the team or teams he played for. To be elected, a candidate has to be named on at least 75% of the ballots sent out January 5th each year.

Although the Hall was not opened until 1939, the first election was held in 1936. Five of baseball's all-time greatest stars were inducted: Babe Ruth, Ty Cobb, Honus (Hans) Wagner, Christy Mathewson, and Walter Johnson. Every year since then has marked the election of such stars as Rube Marquard, Napoleon LaJoie, Tris Speaker, Lefty Grove, Jimmy Foxx, Ted Williams, Joe DiMaggio, Sandy Koufax, Jackie Robinson, Willie Mays, Roberto Clemente, and many others who have joined those first five.

Many decades of organized pro baseball went by before blacks were accepted into the game. Blacks played on their own circuits, called the Negro Leagues. Many of them were so outstanding that recently a special category for players from those leagues was added to the Hall of Fame. Records of their playing days were sketchy at best, but they were admitted to the Hall on the basis of reliable accounts of people who saw them play, and from stories in the Negro press.

A special section was also reserved for managers, umpires, and baseball owners and executives who were deserving of election to the Hall.

Lifelike bronze heads of all the members adorn the beautiful Hall of Fame gallery. Colorful, historical displays of old-time photos, equipment, and uniforms are in abundance. There are mementos such as the spikes worn by Ty Cobb, the greatest career base stealer of all time; one of Babe Ruth's bats; gloves

The Hall of Fame Gallery:
a bronze plaque of every member in the Hall.

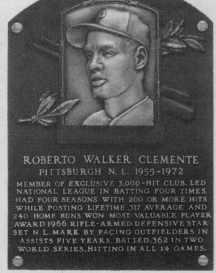

THEODORE SAMUEL WILLIAMS
"TED"
BOSTON RED SOX A.L. 1939-1960
BATTED .406 IN 1941. LED A.L. IN BATTING
6 TIMES; SLUGGING PERCENTAGE 9 TIMES;
TOTAL BASES 6 TIMES; RUNS SCORED 6 TIMES;
BASES ON BALLS 8 TIMES. TOTAL HITS 2654
INCLUDED 521 HOME RUNS. LIFETIME BATTING
AVERAGE .344; LIFETIME SLUGGING AVERAGE
.634. MOST VALUABLE A.L. PLAYER 1946 & 1949.
PLAYED IN 18 ALL STAR GAMES. NAMED PLAYER
OF THE DECADE 1951-1960.

ROBERTO WALKER CLEMENTE
PITTSBURGH N.L. 1955-1972
MEMBER OF EXCLUSIVE 3,000-HIT CLUB. LED
NATIONAL LEAGUE IN BATTING FOUR TIMES.
HAD FOUR SEASONS WITH 200 OR MORE HITS
WHILE POSTING LIFETIME .317 AVERAGE AND
240 HOME RUNS. WON MOST VALUABLE PLAYER
AWARD 1966. RIFLE-ARMED DEFENSIVE STAR
SET N.L. MARK BY PACING OUTFIELDERS IN
ASSISTS FIVE YEARS. BATTED .362 IN TWO
WORLD SERIES, HITTING IN ALL 14 GAMES.

Bronze busts of Ted Williams and Roberto Clemente.

worn by some of the greatest fielders. More than 1,000 items are on display. There are even special free movies, including one exclusively on Babe Ruth, which enhance the history of the game. There is a special World Series room that traces the history and highlights of the great Fall Classic. Almost a quarter of a million visitors a year flock to the Cooperstown Hall of Fame—and nobody has ever been disappointed.

The museum is, indeed, a fitting tribute to the almost 200 players, managers, umpires, and officials who are enshrined there.

OUTFIELDERS

The One and Only Bambino

Babe Ruth, outfielder, NY Yankees, 1919–1934, elected 1936.

His name was George Herman Ruth, and he grew up in a Baltimore orphanage, where he first played baseball. Later he would simply be known as Babe Ruth, and as such he would become the most famous player in the history of the game—one of the most famous names in all of sports. In fact, one of the most famous Americans of all time.

He became known by other names: the Sultan of Swat, the Bambino. But always he was known as the man who hit home runs. He was the man who paved the way for new glamor and new excitement in baseball with the art of hitting the ball out of the park.

Before Babe Ruth, the home run was pretty much a rarity. A player named Frank Baker of the Philadelphia A's was called Home Run Baker because he hit a dozen a season. That was big homer production in the early years of the 20th century. Then along came Babe Ruth, who showed the hitters how they could swing for the fences.

The homers began flying out of the park on May 6, 1915. Babe Ruth was a lefty pitcher for the Boston Red Sox, and they were playing the Yankees in the Polo Grounds in New York (before Yankee Stadium was built). Ruth came to bat in the third inning. There was a mighty *swoosh!* and the ball sailed into the upper deck in right field. There would be 713 more after that until Babe Ruth stood alone on the all-time home-run list—but a man named Hank Aaron changed things in 1974.

Courtesy of the International Museum of Photography, Rochester, NY.

Ruth's homer saga, however, began in the Baltimore orphanage. He was a big kid, known as Big George when only 15. The minor league Baltimore Orioles heard about his prowess on the St. Mary's Industrial Home team, and when he was 19 they convinced Brother Gilbert, who ran the home, to let the youngster be adopted by the Orioles and play ball for them. They would pay him the sum of $600 a year.

It took the big league scouts just a few weeks to discover him, and the Boston Red Sox bought him for $2,900. The youthful southpaw was an instant pitching success and would surely have gone on to pitching super–stardom—except for one thing. He began hitting the ball out of the park, and the Red Sox started using him occasionally in the outfield to take advantage of his bat. By 1919, he had set a new big league mark of 29 homers. But the Sox needed money and sold Ruth to the Yankees that year for a whopping (then) $125,000.

With the Yanks, Ruth was soon strictly an outfielder—and a good one—and his homer production began to soar. When the Yanks built their own stadium in 1923 it was called "The House that Ruth Built." It certainly was. Fans flocked to see the powerful slugger, not only in New York but around the league. In 1920, he hit 54 homers. The whole nation was focused on what Ruth's limits might be. Many of his blasts were deep into the stands. Nobody had seen such slugging. In 1927, he blasted 60, and everyone knew it would be an all-time mark—unless Ruth, himself, broke it. Later, Roger Maris of the Yankees would hit 61, but in an extended season of 160 games as opposed to the earlier seasons of 154. Ruth's batting averages were just as spectacular. One year, .358, another, .378. He would end up with a brilliant .342, lifetime. He led the league in homers 10 times.

Baseball was Babe Ruth. Babe Ruth was baseball. Everything he did, off or on the field, was news. He had no use for training rules. He was just a big, fun-loving guy. (He had gotten the nickname Babe in Boston.) He ate tremendous meals, and they were reported in the press. Babe Ruth was the idol of millions, and he became the hub around which the mighty Yankee dynasty was built. Politicians struggled to shake his hand and have their pictures taken with him.

In the late 1920s, when he sought a salary of $80,000 a year—unheard of at the time—a reporter asked Ruth how he could expect a higher salary than the president of the United States. "Easy," said Ruth, "I had a better year than he did."

Baseball fans all over the nation agreed, and Babe Ruth got his raise.

He was the stuff of which legends are truly made. In the 1932 World Series against the Chicago Cubs, the Cubs' pitcher got two strikes on him. Ruth stepped back a bit and pointed toward right field. Thousands in the stands knew what he meant. On the next pitch, Babe Ruth blasted the ball out of the park.

But Babe Ruth wanted to manage the Yanks. He insisted he be given the chance. The club refused his demand and, in reply, dealt him to the Boston Braves in his last season. Ruth was insulted. So were his fans. He only played for the Braves a few weeks and retired.

There was no way Babe Ruth, big Number 3, could not be voted into the Hall of Fame in 1936, the first year of the selections.

Perhaps the Greatest All-Around Star

Ty Cobb, outfielder, Detroit Tigers, 1905–1928, elected 1936.

It was August 30, 1905. Old Bennett Field in Detroit. Two men were on for the Tigers. Jack Chesbro, pitching for the New York Highlanders (later called the Yankees), had won 41 games the year before and was having another great year. He smiled coolly at the grim, tight-lipped 18-year-old kid, a pinchhitter, at bat for the first time in his big league career.

The kid looked tough and mean as he gripped his bat, lefty. Right hand low, left hand high on the handle. The kid was Tyrus Raymond Cobb, just up from Augusta in South Atlantic League. Chesbro laughed at the kid. The kid's mouth twisted in a snarl. He spat out some nasty words. *Bush-league kid!* thought Chesbro. He pumped and threw. The bush-league kid swung and drilled a screaming double to right field, driving in two runs.

From second base the kid glared savagely at Chesbro. A lot of big leaguers would get to know and fear that glare.

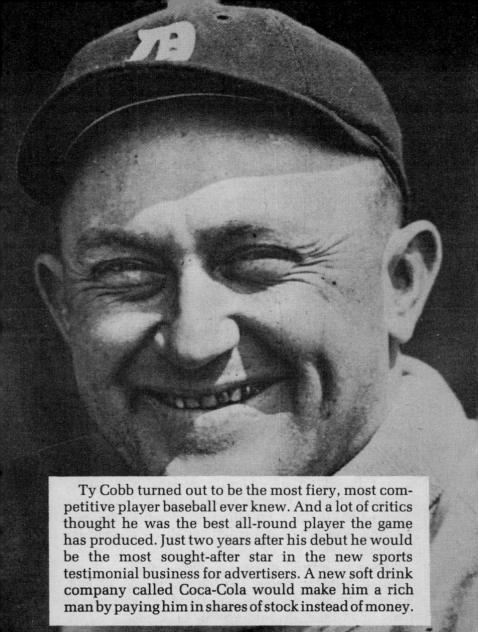

Ty Cobb turned out to be the most fiery, most competitive player baseball ever knew. And a lot of critics thought he was the best all-round player the game has produced. Just two years after his debut he would be the most sought-after star in the new sports testimonial business for advertisers. A new soft drink company called Coca-Cola would make him a rich man by paying him in shares of stock instead of money.

In 1909, four years after breaking in, he had become baseball's first modern superstar. In addition to stealing 76 bases that year (incredible then, but soon he would do better) he won the AL batting crown with .377, led with 216 hits, 116 runs, 107 runs batted in, a slugging average of .517, and 9 home runs. (It was a day when the majors used the so-called "dead ball," and swinging for the fences was not yet stylish.)

He was probably most famed for his baserunning. He once told in his own words how he stole home in a World Series game against the Pirates. He stole home 20 times in his career, more than anyone in history.

"There was a relief pitcher in, and I figured he'd give little thought to me at third. His mind would be on the batter and his ability to get the ball over. I walked some distance off third to see if he was paying me any attention. He was looking at his catcher. I turned back toward third to disarm the catcher.

"Then, just as the pitcher raised his arm in his preliminary motion I dashed for the plate. A right-hander was up so I had some protection, and in sliding I threw my body away from the plate, giving the catcher only my foot to tag in case he got the ball in time. I ripped the ground for three feet with my spikes before I touched the plate, but I made it. I'd have been called crazy if I'd failed—in a World Series—but the way I had it figured left little chance for failure."

Before he retired in 1928 at age 42, with 24 years with Detroit, the Georgia Peach, as he was known, set more records than any man ever to play the game. Only one of them would ever be broken.

Cobb played in the most games (3,034), got the most hits (4,191), and scored the most runs (2,245). He stole the most bases (892) and his 96 in 1916 stood as a record for 47 years until Lou Brock of the Cardinals broke it with 118. (Rickey Henderson's 130 set a new record in 1982.)

His lifetime batting average of .367 is still the record. He won his first league batting crown in 1907 and repeated it for the next eight seasons.

In eight seasons he had more than 200 hits per year—another mark. In 1911, when he hit .420, he got 248 hits in 591 times at bat—threatening to get a hit almost every other time at the plate.

There were other records in his remarkable list of achievements, including three seasons of hitting .400 or better.

In addition to his records, Ty Cobb would be famed as the man who developed the hook slide, the fade-away and fall-away slides to give the fielder less chance to tag him. It was fitting that when baseball's Hall of Fame opened in Cooperstown, the first thing put on display was a pair of Ty Cobb's gleaming spiked shoes.

Tris Speaker, outfielder, Cleveland Indians, 1907–1928, elected 1937.

A super center fielder for the Indians, who later managed the Tribe, Speaker changed the game by often playing shallow, enabling him to pick off line drives and throw out base runners . . . His 449 assists are a record for outfielders . . . Twice he tossed

out 35 runners in a single season, an AL record . . .
Also a great hitter, once led league with .386 with a
lifetime .344 . . . Not a leading homer hitter (115), he
did hit more doubles (793) than any player in history.

Willie Keeler, outfielder, original Baltimore Orioles, 1892–1910, elected 1939.

Before the turn of the century, Willie Keeler played
with the original Baltimore Orioles, who were not in
the majors after formation of American and National
Leagues . . . Known as Wee Willie because at only
5-4½ he was easily the smallest superstar of big-time
baseball . . . Eight years in a row he collected 200 hits
or more, also hit in first 44 games of 1897 season . .
Rarely hit for distance, but his slogan was, "Hit 'em
where they ain't." He drove pitchers and fielders
crazy in becoming game's finest place-hitter . . . Lifetime was .345.

Mel Ott, outfielder, New York Giants, 1926–1947, elected 1951.

Mel Ott was already famous before he became a
star—by joining the Giants in 1925 when only 16
years old . . . He saw service both as a catcher and
outfielder, but his claim to fame lay in his hitting . . .

A little guy, only 5-9 and 165 pounds, he had a weird stance at the plate, lifting his right leg just before swinging . . . He seemed to go on forever, playing 22 seasons and becoming 12th on the all-time homer list with 511, hitting 30 or more in eight different years.

Paul Waner, outfielder, Pittsburgh Pirates, 1926–1942, elected 1952; Lloyd Waner, outfielder, Pirates, 1927–1945, elected 1967.

Paul was known as Big Poison Waner, and was the older of the two Waner brothers who starred in the same Pirate outfield . . . He was Big Poison to Little Poison Lloyd, only because he was older by three years . . . Both were small-sized, 5-8 and 5-9 respectively . . . Both were giant-sized in their baseball abilities, which made them the only modern brother act in the Hall of Fame . . . Both could beat you in a half dozen different ways and did it throughout their long careers . . . Hitting, throwing, fielding, stealing, and thinking . . . Neither was a long-ball hitter, but both sprayed line drives to all fields . . . Paul made the exclusive 3,000-hit club, won three NL batting crowns, hit .300 or more 14 times, and lashed 200 or more hits eight times on his way to a career .333 . . . Lloyd hit .355 as a rookie, with 223 hits his first year—still a record for rookies . . . He batted .300 or better in 10 of his first 12 years, wound up with .316 lifetime.

Harry Heilmann, outfielder, Detroit Tigers, 1914–31, elected 1952.

Heilmann, a brilliant student of the game as well as a player, went on to a great career as a baseball broadcaster . . . But first he established himself as one of the best right-handed hitters of all time . . . Not too productive in homers, he was a slashing batsman who won four AL batting titles in the early and mid-1920s with marks of .394, .403, .393, and .398 . . . Although a teammate for a few years with the great Ty Cobb, they never produced a pennant for the Tigers.

Al Simmons, outfielder, Philadelphia Athletics and six other clubs, 1924–1944, elected 1953.

A sensational hitter for the oft-time championship A's, Simmons just missed joining the 3,000-hit club, swatting 2,927, making him second among righties only to Hall of Famer Al Kaline's 3,007 . . . His "foot-in-the-bucket" (withdrawing one foot back toward dugout) made experts scoff at his chances of making the big leagues, but his weird stance produced a lifetime .334, 307 homers, and 539 doubles . . . Also a dependable fielder.

Heine Manush, outfielder, Detroit Tigers and five other clubs, 1923–1939, elected 1955.

Heine Manush (pronounced Man-OOSH) a big, lefty outfielder, was one of the great hitters of his day . . . Pitchers didn't fear he'd hit a homer (only 110 in his career), but he had a keen batting eye and always got solid wood on the ball, slashing out singles and doubles (491) to all fields . . . Won the 1926 AL batting crown to nose out Babe Ruth on final day of season, with six for nine in a doubleheader . . . Hit .378 again in 1928 but lost crown by one percentage point.

He Had Baseball's Hottest Hitting Streak

Joe DiMaggio, outfielder, New York Yankees, 1936–1950, elected 1955.

A truly great hitter and a superb fielder who was probably the most graceful center fielder of all time, Joe DiMaggio made everything look easy—whether it was stroking an extra base hit or hauling down a drive over his head with one hand. He would have been a Hall of Famer, no matter what. He had come up to the Yankees in 1936 from the Pacific Coast

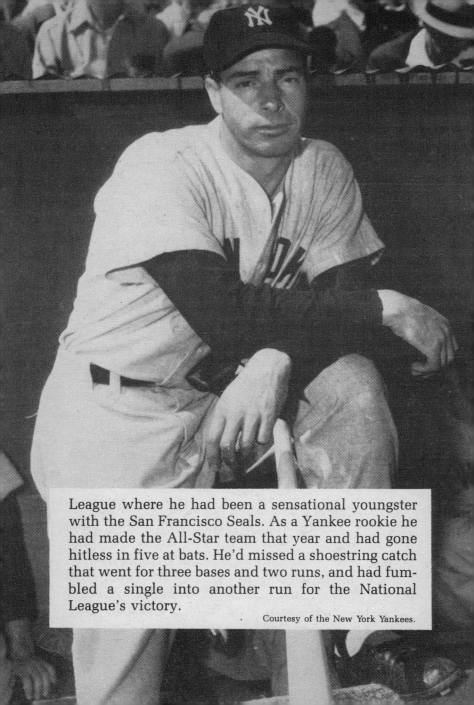

League where he had been a sensational youngster with the San Francisco Seals. As a Yankee rookie he had made the All-Star team that year and had gone hitless in five at bats. He'd missed a shoestring catch that went for three bases and two runs, and had fumbled a single into another run for the National League's victory.

Courtesy of the New York Yankees.

Everyone soon forgot all that as he went on to super-stardom. But it was what happened in 1941 that forever cemented his fame.

There was no great stir when DiMaggio got a single in four at bats on May 15, 1941, and no great commotion next day when he got a homer and triple. But reporters began to take notice when he'd hit safely in ten straight games.

Now he was on a hitting streak that gripped the whole sports world. Tension for DiMaggio, the fans, and the official scorers began to mount. Was it a hit . . . or an error? The scorers' judgment began to be on trial. On June 3, he hit a single against Detroit: 20 straight. On June 10: 25 straight. On June 20, he tied the National League mark of 33 set by the great Rogers Hornsby. On June 28, his two hits against Philadelphia tied George Sisler's American League mark of 41. And the next day he set a new mark of 42.

Fans were wondering now. How long could he continue? Soon enough, the pitchers would stop him— or great fielding.

On July 2, DiMaggio smacked a homer against the Red Sox, making it 45 games in a row. On July 11, a homer and three singles gave him 50 straight games with a hit.

Fans were now going wild, storming the ball parks to see Jolting Joe DiMaggio extend his streak—or be there to see it stopped.

On July 17th, 1941, 67,468 jammed into a night game in Cleveland. He'd gotten three hits the day before for his 56th straight game. Now, his first time up, he hit a screamer down third. Ken Keltner, the

Tribe's great third sacker, made a brilliant stop and threw him out. Joe walked the next time. His third time up, DiMaggio hit another scorcher down third. The ball was going past Keltner, but he made a great stab, snagged the ball, and threw DiMaggio out.

Against Jim Bagby, a relief pitcher, in the eighth inning, DiMaggio hit a crazily bounding grounder to short. Lou Boudreau, the Tribe's shortstop, took it and turned it into a double play.

Joe DiMaggio's streak was over. He had hit safely in 56 straight games. No one has even come close to that mark since. A lot of fans say nobody will ever break it. Who knows? But it is still one of the more remarkable records on the books.

DiMaggio went on to hit 361 homers lifetime and had a shiny .325 lifetime average. But he'll always be remembered most for hitting safely in 56 straight games.

Wahoo Sam Crawford, outfielder, Detroit Tigers, 1899–1917, elected 1957.

When Crawford hung up his spikes in 1917, the Tigers' star outfielder was only 36 hits short of membership in the exclusive 3,000-hit club . . . A fine fielder and a power hitter, he only hit 95 homers, but he had a knack for clubbing out three-base hits, and his 312 lifetime triples is the major league all-time record . . . He had a career batting mark of .309 and was dangerous on the base paths after getting aboard . . . He had 367 career steals and depended more on his knowledge of pitching moves rather than speed.

Zack Wheat, outfielder, Brooklyn Dodgers, 1909–1927, elected 1959.

Fame consists of many things . . . Zack Wheat, who won the NL batting crown in 1918 with mark of .335, did it without hitting a single homer . . . In an 18-year career with the Dodgers (previously called Brooklyn Superbas) he was a brilliant fielder with a strong arm . . . Fourteen times he hit more than .300 for the season and posted a lifetime mark of .317, with 132 homers overall.

Max Carey, outfielder, Pittsburgh Pirates, 1910–1929, elected 1961.

Slender Max Carey could run like a gazelle and was one of baseball's greatest base stealers . . . Ten times he led the National League in thefts (a major league mark) and in one season—1922—he swiped 51 in 53 efforts, the best big league percentage ever for a single season . . . Carey was also a fleet ball hawk with a whiplike throwing arm . . . Not a long ball hitter, but he posted a fine career average of .285 and had six seasons of .300 or better.

Edd Roush, outfielder, Cincinnati, 1913–1931, elected 1962.

Swift, covering great ground, and with a mighty arm, Roush was one of the best outfielders of his day, but achieved his greatest fame with his bat, which, incidentally, was probably the heaviest in the majors (48 ounces) . . . Twice won National League batting crown, hit for .340 or better in a 10-year period, with a career mark of .323 . . . Never a big homer threat (only 67 lifetime) but pitchers feared him with men in scoring position.

Elmer Flick, outfielder, Philadelphia Phillies/Cleveland Naps, 1898–1910, elected 1963.

Elmer Flick was no flake and no fake . . . Early in the 20th century, his hitting drove terror into pitchers' hearts . . . Flick, a fleet outfielder, was a slashing hitter who hit the long ball in his 11-year career (.315 lifetime), hitting 46 homers, 268 doubles, and 170 triples—and speed is the important thing in three-base hits . . . He hit .378 with the Phils one year and, later with the Naps, won the AL crown.

Sam Rice, outfielder, Washington Senators, 1915–1934, elected 1963.

Anyone who plays in the majors 20 years has to be something special . . . Sam Rice did that for the

Washington Senators, and in all but five of his years with them, he hit more than .300 . . . Lifetime he hit a spanking .322 with a high of .350 in 1925 . . . A swift ballhawk, Rice was just as rapid on the base paths and was often among the AL leaders in stolen bases, winning the crown once with 63.

Ted Williams, outfielder, Boston Red Sox, 1939–1961, elected 1966.

They called him the Splendid Splinter because of his tall, slender build—but he was a stout oak at the plate. Umpires secretly agreed that if Ted Williams didn't swing at a pitch it was a ball, because he had the best batting eye in baseball.

A star from the moment he came up to the Red Sox from the Pacific Coast League in 1939, Williams was a good if not great outfielder, but his hitting was legendary. He was the only .400 hitter in more than 35 years of big league play and won the AL batting crown five times. Lifetime he hit .344 and his 521 homers put him eighth in the all-time home-run list. If he hadn't been called to military service as a fighter pilot in World War II and again in the Korean War, he may have challenged Babe Ruth's mark of 714, but his six wartime years wrecked his chances.

In 1941, when he batted his sensational .406 in only his third major league campaign, he was an even .400 on the last day of the season (a doubleheader). When it was suggested that he sit out that final day to protect his .400 he said, grimly: "Not a chance. That would be a cheap way of getting it. I'll play!"

He did and got four hits the first game (including a homer) and two in the second to raise his mark to .406.

Goose Goslin, outfielder, Washington Senators/Detroit Tigers, 1921–1934, elected 1968.

Smallish but compact (5-10, 170), Goslin was one of the best hitters of modern days, as well as a fine left fielder . . . In the heyday of the Senators (and later with the Tigers), Goslin's bat helped Washington to three pennants and the Tigers to two . . . Important in his .316 lifetime were lots of long-ball heroics— 500 doubles, 173 triples, and 248 homers . . . He hit .300 or better 11 seasons.

Kiki Cuyler, outfielder, Pittsburgh Pirates, 1921–1938, elected 1968.

Cuyler had a terrific arm and nifty ball-hawking talent in the outfield and was just as valuable offensively as a hitter and base stealer . . . Four times hit .350 or better and lifetime was .321 . . . He was daring on the base paths and four times led National League in stolen bases . . . Rarely was he ever picked off and often stole third, a difficult feat . . . He starred in four pennant-winning years for the Pirates.

Joe Medwick, outfielder, St. Louis Cardinals, 1932–1947, elected 1968.

Medwick had a funny waddle when playing in the minors and came to the majors with the nickname Ducky . . . One of the stars of the Cards' scrappy Gas House Gang, of the mid-1930s, his fielding was first-rate and his hitting was super . . . Hit .300 or more 14 times and won the triple crown (average, hits, and homers) in 1937, with a mighty .374 average.

Stan Musial, outfielder, St. Louis Cardinals, 1941–1963, elected 1969.

A failure in the minors as a pitcher, the Cardinals switched Musial to the outfield, and he became one of the all-time greats, particularly as a hitter . . . In his 22 years with the Cards, his 3,026 games played was second among Hall of Famers only to Ty Cobb's 3,034 . . . He hit .300 or better 18 times and won NL batting crown seven times . . . Known for his twisted, corkscrew batting stance, he hit 475 career homers and had a lifetime average of .331.

Earle Combs, outfielder, New York Yankees, 1924–1935, elected 1970.

Combs was the center fielder on the World Series champion Yankees of 1927, considered by many the greatest club of all (Ruth, Gehrig, Lazzeri were on that club) . . . With a keen batting eye, he drew average of 70 walks per season at his peak as leadoff batter, and hit a dandy .325 lifetime . . . His fine speed made him a real ball hawk and base stealer, and he was among leaders in putouts and thefts every year.

Chick Hafey, outfielder, St. Louis Cardinals/Cincinnati Reds, 1924–1937, elected 1971.

A dependable and often brilliant fly chaser, Hafey was even better known for his hitting—even though his eyesight was said to be sub-par . . . Finally, he became one of the first major leaguers to wear glasses . . . He had always been a .300 hitter, but he got better as he adjusted to the specs . . . He had six straight seasons batting better than .325 and one year took the NL crown with .349 . . . He shares the league mark of 10 straight hits, and he batted .317 lifetime.

Harry Hooper, outfielder, Boston Red Sox, 1909–1925, elected 1971.

Hall of Famers who hit only .289 lifetime are uncommon, but Hooper was such a dependable, all-around player he couldn't be left out . . . When the

Red Sox were establishing a dynasty in the early 1900s, Hooper was their super right fielder and a leadoff batter who often started things rolling . . . He had a rifle arm and runners hesitated taking an extra base on him . . . He is said to be the first outfielder to use sunglasses.

Monte Irvin, outfielder, Negro Leagues/ New York Giants/Baltimore Orioles/Chicago Cubs, 1949–1954, elected 1971.

Irvin came to the Giants in 1949 after several years of stardom in the Negro Leagues, but in the few years he performed in the majors he proved he could have been an all-star if he'd come to the big leagues sooner . . . A graceful fielder with a strong arm, he also made his presence felt at bat . . . In 1951, he hit 24 homers and had 121 RBIs while batting .312, and was a big reason why the Giants won the NL flag.

Ross Youngs, outfielder, New York Giants, 1917–1926, elected 1972.

Although he was only 30 when he died of a kidney ailment, Youngs had already left his mark in an all-too-short career with the Giants . . . A squat, aggressive hustler, Youngs was admired throughout the NL as a talented fielder, a fiery base runner, and a slashing hitter . . . In seven straight years, he batted .300 or more on his way to a career .322 and three times led National League outfielders in assists.

Brilliant Career Halted by Tragedy

Roberto Clemente, outfielder, Pittsburgh Pirates, 1955–1972, elected 1973.

At the start of the 1972 season, Roberto Clemente, the Pirates' great right fielder, had 2,882 hits, only 118 away from the magic number of 3,000. In all the years baseball had been played by thousands of players, up to that time only ten had reached that almost unreachable level. Clemente had missed 50 games that year with illness and injury. Now, with just two games left at the end of the season, he had 2,999 hits. The whole world awaited the outcome of those two games.

Baseball is more than a sport. Baseball can also be high drama. Nobody could even dream of the kind of drama Roberto Clemente would provide . . .

First of all, he was one of the greatest all-around players of all time. In his 18 years with the Pirates, he was in the all-time top ten in National League games, at bats, hits, singles, and total bases. He had won 12 Gold Glove awards for his fielding. Once, in 1967, he had set an NL record of ten straight hits in two games. He'd been only the second player in history to hit safely in all the games of two seven-game World Series.

He was noted for his acrobatic fielding—making diving and shoestring catches, making catches while bouncing off outfield walls, or reaching into the stands. He played every game as though 100% would never be enough.

Born and raised in Puerto Rico, he was a high school track star so good that his coaches were pointing him toward the Olympics. But his real love was baseball.

As a 17-year-old he played for Santurce in the fast Puerto League big leagues, where a Dodger scout saw him and signed him. Sent in 1954 to the Dodgers' Montreal farm team in the International League, he impressed the Dodger management—but the Dodgers lost him due to a technicality on ownership rules, and he went into the draft of minor league players. The Pirates grabbed him, and in 1955 the 20-year-old rookie was an immediate sensation with Pittsburgh.

He was the big reason why the second division Pirates began the climb to pennant contenders. It took a few years, but by 1960 the Pirates had won their first NL pennant in 33 years. They beat the Yankees in the World Series. Along the way, Clemente made the year's greatest catch. He raced over for a Willie Mays drive, speared it after a long run, and crashed into a concrete wall. Blood poured from his face, but he held the ball. He spent the next six days in the hospital.

With Roberto leading the way, the Pirates captured their division titles in 1970, '71, and '72, won the NL flag in 1971, and defeated Baltimore in the World Series.

It was the following season that Roberto Clemente took the stage in high drama—his quest to join the 3,000-hit club.

With 2,999 hits to his credit and two games left in the 1972 season, Clemente faced the New York Mets' great Tom Seaver in the Pirates' home field. The park was jammed. The whole baseball word awaited news from Pittsburgh. Would Clemente make his 3,000th this season, with time running out?

In the first inning he hit a grounder off Seaver's glove. The Mets' second baseman tried to field it, and it glanced off his glove. Clemente was on first, but the scoreboard flashed an *H* for hit, and the crowd roared. But immediately the sign changed to *E* for error. The official scorer had changed his mind on his decision. Roberto didn't get a hit the rest of the game.

Following the game, reporters asked him what he thought of the decision on the ground ball in the first inning. "I wouldn't have wanted the scorer to call it a hit if he weren't sure of it," said Roberto. "I don't want my 3,000th hit to be a cheap gift. I want to earn it, so there's no doubt in anyone's mind."

So there he was, one hit away on the last day of the season. And Clemente was facing the Mets' Jon Matlack, who hadn't allowed him a hit in the several games he'd pitched against him that year. If the jinx held, Clemente would have to wait until next season to get his 3,000th.

A few minutes after 3:00 P.M. next day, the suspense was ended. Clemente swung at a Matlack curve and slammed the ball to deep left center for a double. Standing on second base he got the loudest ovation in the history of Pirate baseball. He had his 3,000th hit.

No one could guess there would never be another game, another season for Clemente to reach that number if he had failed in this season finale. There was an earthquake in Nicaragua that following winter. The Central American nation was devastated. Relief came from all over the world. On the morning of December 31, 1972, Roberto Clemente supervised the loading of food and supplies aboard an airplane at San Juan. He had chartered the plane and collected the supplies himself for this mercy mission to Nicaragua. He was going to go along, personally, to see that everything was distributed properly.

Two minutes after the plane took off, there were three explosions aboard. It nosed over and plunged into the sea. Everyone was killed—including Roberto Clemente, whose dramatic 3,000th hit in the last game he'd ever play was surely one of the high spots in the entire history of baseball.

Rules for election in Baseball's Hall of Fame require a player to be out of baseball for five years before he can be voted upon. They changed the rules for Roberto Clemente and held a special election. He was unanimously elected to Cooperstown, and everyone agreed he belonged—without waiting.

Mickey Mantle, outfielder, New York Yankees, 1951–1964, elected 1974.

Mantle came up as a shortstop but was quickly shifted to the outfield, where his speed made him the ideal center fielder . . . As a star of the Yanks' many flag winners in the 1950s–'60s, he just missed the magic .300 lifetime (.289), but he was a tremendous hitter—slamming 536 homers, and hitting .300 or better ten seasons . . . Many of his homers went for tremendous distance and his 18 in World Series play is highest in history.

Earl Averill, outfielder, Cleveland Indians, 1929–1941, elected 1975.

Averill is the only Hall of Famer who hit a homer in his first big league at bat and went on to hit .333 as a rookie ... Smallish at 5-9 and 170, he had a smooth swing that gave him great power as he hit .300 or better in eight seasons, including 238 homers, 128 triples, and 401 doubles ... Called the Earl of Snohomish (Wash.), he was a graceful fielder and batted .318 lifetime ... In his second year he had three homers in one game and missed a fourth by a foot.

Ralph Kiner, outfielder, Pittsburg Pirates, 1946–1955, elected 1975.

Recently a successful baseball broadcaster, Kiner's major league career was hampered and shortened by injuries ... But in his 10 years with the Pirates, Kiner established himself as a genuine batting star as well as being a fine fielder ... Although his career batting average of .279 is lowest among Hall of Fame outfielders, he hit 369 homers ... Came close to the magic 60 with 54 in 1949, and won or shared NL homer crown in each of his first seven years with Pirates ... His ratio of 7.1 homers per 100 times at bat is second only to Ruth's.

Hack Wilson, outfielder, New York Giants/ Chicago Cubs/Brooklyn Dodgers, 1923– 1934, elected 1979.

The shortest, chunkiest (5-6, 195) outfielder in the Hall, Hack Wilson was a fair enough fielder but it was his bat that delivered him to lasting fame . . . In 12 years with the Cubs he hit for .307, but every time he went to the plate he was a potential homer hitter . . . He had 244 in his career . . . In 1930 he had a season that was sensational: 56 homers (highest ever in the NL); 190 runs batted in (highest ever in the majors); .356 average.

The "Say, Hey!" Kid

Willie Mays, outfielder, New York and San Francisco Giants/New York Mets, 1951–1974, elected 1979.

It would go down in history as the greatest catch ever made in a World Series game. It is still talked about.

The New York Giants were playing the Cleveland Indians at the old Polo Grounds in New York, in the first game of the Series of 1954. The Indians, who had won 113 of their (then) 154-game schedule (an American League record), were heavily favored.

The game was tied, 2–2, in the eighth, and the Tribe had two men on base. At the plate was Vic Wertz, their big slugger. Wertz already had tripled earlier.

In came the pitch and Wertz slammed it far and high to dead center. As soon as the ball left the bat, Willie Mays, the Giants' young outfielder, knew it was heading for the wall beneath the bleachers. Turning his back on the ball he raced swiftly toward the wall, hoping the ball wouldn't clear it. If he played it off the wall maybe he could hold the Indians to just one run. After racing more than 100 feet he turned to look for the ball over his shoulder and got a glimpse of it as it was flying over his head.

With the ball beginning descent ahead of him, his back to home plate, he reached out like a fleet receiver in football and gathered it in. Nobody in baseball had ever seen anything like it. The Indians' runner on third scored after the catch. The runner on second might have scored, too, because it had been a tremendously long fly. But in a blazing instant, Willie Mays had whirled around with his catch and fired the greatest throw of his career. The ball arrived at the catcher, more than 350 feet away, on one hop. The Indians' runner, still dumbfounded by the catch, remained at third.

The Giants went on to win the game and sweep Cleveland four straight for the world championship. Most people agreed that the Indians never recovered from Willie Mays's dramatic catch and lost all their confidence.

Leo Durocher, the Giants' manager who had been in baseball 40 years as player and manager, said Willie Mays was the greatest player he ever saw.

Mays's greatness was in his fire and his incredible versatility. He could hit. His fielding was superb. He was one of the great base runners of his day. He had a cannon for an arm. And he could inspire his teammates with confidence.

Willie's road to the Hall of Fame was set from the start. His father, a steelworker, played ball for a local Negro Leagues team in Birmingham, Ala. Every night, from the time Willie was five, they played catch in the backyard. When Willie was nine he played with boys 13. In 1941 when Joe DiMaggio was on his famous 56-game hitting streak, little Willie was glued to the radio every night to hear if the streak was still alive. DiMaggio was his idol, and Willie dreamed some day of being a star center fielder, too.

He starred in football, basketball, and baseball in high school. One night his father told him the Birmingham Barons of the Negro Leagues wanted him to come to a tryout. The 16-year-old sprayed hits all over the field and was soon the youngest player in the Negro Leagues and traveled all over the South and East.

A New York Giant scout saw him and immediately signed him. Willie started with Trenton, N.J., a Giants' farm club. In 81 games he hit .353. In 1951 (already known as the "Say, Hey!" Kid, because he started so many conversations that way), the Giants promoted him to Minneapolis in the American Association. He tore up the league. In 35 games he hit .427 and hit eight homers. He hit a line drive so hard the ball made a hole in the wooden outfield fence.

The Giants lost no time in sending for him. Trailing the Dodgers by 13½ games in August, the Giants got a lift from the young rookie. His bat took them on a tide of victory. At the end of the season they were tied with the Dodgers and beat them in a special three-game playoff. It was Bobby Thomson's famous home run that clinched it, but it was young Willie Mays who was now the star of the team. He had hit 20 homers and was Rookie of the Year.

Drafted into the army the following year (the Korean War was on) he served at Fort Eustice, Va., where he also developed his famous "basket catch." When he rejoined the Giants the next year, he startled the league with his style. He held his hands in front of him, waist high, and simply let a fly ball fall into them. It drove Manager Leo Durocher crazy, but Willie was comfortable with it.

By 1954 Willie was the most electrifying player in baseball. He led the NL in batting (.345) and slammed 42 homers. For four straight playing years he led the league in stolen bases. Naturally, he was the league's MVP. He was an amazingly complete player, and all New Yorkers loved him. When the Giants shifted to San Francisco, all Westerners loved him. In 1961, he hit four homers in one game against the Braves. He always thought he'd have hit a record fifth, but the man ahead of him in the batting order made the last out of the ninth inning.

In 1972, his talents aging, he was traded back to New York with the Mets. But there was one bit of drama left in him. When the San Francisco Giants came to town to play the Mets, Willie in his first at bat smashed a homer against the club that had cut him loose. Many of his fans thought it had to be the most satisfying of his career—a career in which he hit 586 homers—putting him third on the all-time list behind Babe Ruth and Hank Aaron. But he'll always be remembered more for the most incredible catch ever made in a World Series.

Chuck Klein, outfielder, Philadelphia Phillies, 1928–1944, elected 1980.

Chuck Klein never played for a perennial contender, as he was with the then-lowly Phillies, but was a great performer on his own . . . A brilliant fielder, he still holds big league mark for assists by an out-fielder, 44 in 1930 . . . Was the NL triple crown winner (homers, hits, runs batted in) in 1932 . . . In one year he hit .386, 40 homers, and 170 RBIs but, amazingly, didn't lead league in any category . . . His career batting average was .320.

Al Kaline, outfielder, Detroit Tigers, 1953–1968, elected 1980.

Kaline gave early promise of greatness by winning the AL batting crown at age 20, with .340, and for 22 years was smooth, super performer with the Tigers . . . He is one of only 15 major leaguers to reach the 3,000-hit club, winding up with 3,007 and a batting average of .297, just three points short of the top-ranked .300 . . . A long-ball hitter, he clubbed 399 homers and 498 doubles—and had a record 18 nominations to the All-Star team.

Duke Snider, outfielder, Brooklyn and Los Angeles Dodgers, 1947–1964, elected 1980.

Snider played in a modern era when pitchers were supreme, but they always had problems with the fans' favorite, The Dook . . . A sweet swinger on any kind of pitch, he batted .295 over a long, 18 season-career, hitting 358 doubles and 407 homers . . . In a stretch of five straight seasons he walloped 40 or more four-baggers . . . Eleven homers in World Series gives him the NL record.

He Smashed Ruth's Record

Henry Aaron, outfielder, Milwaukee and Atlanta Braves, 1954–1977, elected 1982.

Of course, Henry Aaron would have made it to Cooperstown even without that dramatic moment in Atlanta on the night of April 8, 1974. Certainly the moment helped, although everyone knew it was coming.

It was 9:06 P.M. The fourth inning of a game between the Atlanta Braves and Los Angeles Dodgers. In the on-deck circle was Hammerin' Hank. Bad Henry. Pitchers had lots of names for Henry Aaron. More fans were watching him kneeling there than watching Darrell Evans at the plate. The Dodgers were ahead, 3–1. Evans reached first on an error. Now, pitcher Al Downing was facing Henry Aaron.

A few days earlier, on opening day, he'd drilled the ball over the left field wall in Cincinnati for his 714th homer, tying Babe Ruth's all-time record. Now the baseball world wondered how long it would take him to hit his 715th and break the most famous of baseball records. A magic number: 715. Sports fans almost held Ruth's record sacred. A record safe forever.

Now, in Atlanta, Aaron had walked first time up. Fans had booed the pitcher. Millions of TV fans felt the same way. Bad Henry deserved a chance at a decent pitch.

The suspense mounted as Aaron stepped into the batter's box. Downing's first pitch was a ball. The second was a fastball, belt high. Aaron lashed out with his bat. A second later the crowd was roaring as the ball sailed in a high arc to deep left center. Everyone knew it was going over, but Henry's eyes followed the ball every foot of its way. Dodger outfielder Bill Buckner leaped high, but no use. Fireworks exploded in the park, and Henry Aaron's 715th homer was on its way into history.

United Press International Photo

His teammates mobbed him as he crossed home plate. His mother and father leaped from their box seats and raced over to their son and flung their arms around him. The game was held up for 10 minutes as Aaron received awards and listened to speeches he hardly heard. Atlanta relief pitcher Tom House ran in from the bullpen where he had caught Henry's homer and handed him the ball. That ball and Henry were forever joined in baseball lore.

It had all started in Mobile, Ala. A shy youth who preferred reading to sports, he didn't play baseball in high school because the school didn't have a team. But he played sandlot ball and was spotted by a scout for a semipro club, who offered him three dollars a game. A month later a scout for a team in the Negro Leagues saw him and offered him $200 a month to play for the Indianapolis Clowns when he graduated from high school.

A year later his ability had attracted big league attention. The then Boston Braves signed him and farmed him out for two years. It was all upward bound from then on. At age 20, Henry Aaron was the Braves' regular right fielder. He hit 13 homers as a rookie, and the following season hit .314 and 27 homers. By his third year he had won the National League batting crown with .328. He was now an established star, and for seven years he led the league in total bases. Four times he won the league home-run crown, four times the runs-batted-in championship. For 15 straight years he made the league All-Star team.

Aaron was also a brilliant fielder and four times won the prestigious Gold Glove award. Base runners took few chances with his rifle arm. As a runner himself on the bases, he was always a threat to steal and had more than 300 career thefts.

The Braves had moved from Milwaukee to Atlanta halfway through his career, and he was the first black player to be given a "night" in the South. Aaron finished his sensational 23-year major league career having played in 3,298 games and collecting 3,771 hits, putting him well up in the 3,000-hit club. He posted a .305 career batting average—and up there, all by itself, is his mark of 755 home runs—numbers that are the most impressive of all at Cooperstown.

Frank Robinson, outfielder, Cincinnati Reds/Baltimore Orioles/Los Angeles Dodgers/California Angels, 1961–1974, elected 1982.

Robinson was the all-around baseball player— fielder, hitter, and base runner . . . The only man in baseball history to be named MVP in both the National and American Leagues (1961 Reds; 1966 Orioles), Robinson was a superb outfielder and slashing, consistent hitter, with 522 career homers and a lifetime batting mark of .294 . . . The first black manager in the majors, he led the Cleveland Indians and San Francisco Giants.

INFIELDERS

Honus (Hans) Wagner, shortstop, Pittsburgh Pirates, 1897–1917, elected 1936.

There are experts still debating whether Honus Wagner or Ty Cobb was the greatest all-around baseball player of all time . . . Cobb seems to win by an eyelash, but you can't go wrong if you vote for the Pirates' Flying Dutchman. Husky and square-built at 5-11 and 200 pounds, his image belied his grace, speed, and agility . . . He covered an amazing amount of ground in the field, ranging right, left, and deep into the hole to snatch grounders or grabbing line drives . . . His speed also showed up on the base paths, where he stole 720 bases lifetime, and six times led the National League in swipes . . . But his hitting was just as important in building his lasting fame. He was a star as a young player, hitting .344 in his break-in season of 1897 and went on to rack up 17 straight years of .300 or better . . . He won the National League batting crown eight times, and although not a feared homer hitter with only 101 lifetime, he was a power hitter who swatted 252 triples, third highest among Famers, and 651 doubles, fourth highest.

Napoleon LaJoie, second baseman, Philadelphia Phillies/Philadelphia Athletics/Cleveland Indians, 1896–1915, elected 1937.

It's either LaJoie or Rogers Hornsby as the game's greatest second baseman . . . Spent 21 years in the majors, first with the Phillies, then the A's, then with Cleveland, where he attained his greatest stardom . . . Ten times he hit more than .350 and was over .300 for 16 of his 21 campaigns . . . Lifetime he was .339, won three AL batting crowns, and was considered the best infielder of his era.

The "Iron Man" of Baseball

Lou Gehrig, first baseman, New York Yankees, 1925–1939, elected 1939.

Not all great moments in sports have to be exciting. But they can be dramatic or even bittersweet in their significance.

On June 2, 1925, Wally Pipp, first baseman for the New York Yankees, told Manager Miller Huggins that he had a headache. Huggins said: "Okay, take the day off. We'll let the rookie fill in for you."

The rookie, a shy youngster just two years out of Hartford in the Eastern League, played first base that day. Wally Pipp never did get his job back. Lou Geh-

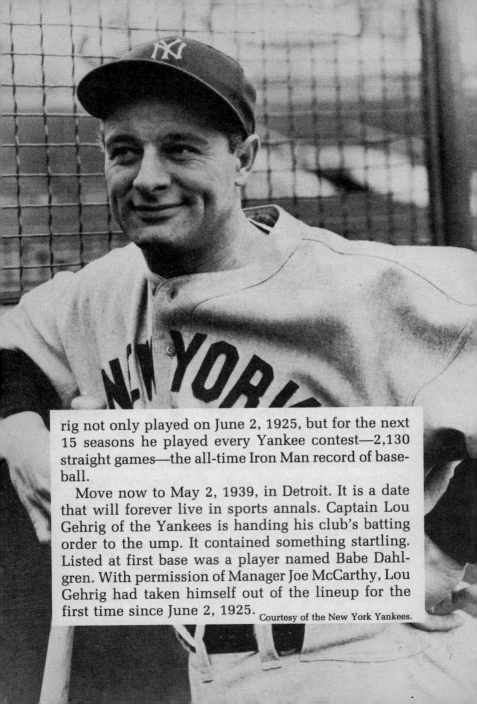

rig not only played on June 2, 1925, but for the next 15 seasons he played every Yankee contest—2,130 straight games—the all-time Iron Man record of base-ball.

Move now to May 2, 1939, in Detroit. It is a date that will forever live in sports annals. Captain Lou Gehrig of the Yankees is handing his club's batting order to the ump. It contained something startling. Listed at first base was a player named Babe Dahl-gren. With permission of Manager Joe McCarthy, Lou Gehrig had taken himself out of the lineup for the first time since June 2, 1925. Courtesy of the New York Yankees.

As the announcement was made, a great cheer of appreciation went up from thousands of Tiger fans. Gehrig tipped his cap to them and went to the bench to sit down.

There had been signs for two years that Gehrig had been slowing down. But he'd never thought of going to the bench. He had too much pride in his playing streak and his desire to help the club. He had been one of the greatest players the game had produced. He was not only a tremendous hitter, always a home run threat, but was a slick fielder at first base. Had he not played in Babe Ruth's shadow, Gehrig would have been the most famous Yankee of all time. His 493 homers put him 13th among all-time homer hitters. He had a glittering career batting mark of .340 and five times led the league in runs batted in.

But mostly Lou Gehrig's fame was due to his consecutive game streak. He played with sprained ankles, sprained wrists, deep bruises, with severe spike wounds, sore throats, punctured blisters. There wasn't much that didn't happen to Gehrig in his 15 seasons as a Yankee. Lesser men would have benched themselves with injuries he shrugged off.

Doctors at first weren't sure what the mysterious illness was that had attacked him two years before he benched himself. But it seemed to affect his coordination slightly. When he finally took himself out of the starting lineup after those 2,130 straight games, he said to reporters: "I just haven't helped the club. I don't want to keep coming up with men on base and not bringing them home . . ." Veteran sports writers felt the sadness within them as they took their notes.

That afternoon, the story was on the front pages all over the nation. Even President Franklin D. Roosevelt was told about it by an aide minutes after the news broke. On July 4, 1939 there was a Lou Gehrig Day at Yankee Stadium. Now it was officially known that the Iron Horse was off the track forever. Doctors now knew his disease was a rare one called amyotrophic lateral sclerosis, which attacked the nervous system and could never be cured. Today it is still called Lou Gehrig's Disease.

More than 60,000 fans watched Lou Gehrig come to the microphone that day at home plate. Surrounded by teammates and former Yankee stars, including Babe Ruth, Gehrig said: "You've been reading about a bad break I got. Yet today I consider myself the luckiest man on the face of the earth . . ."

Gehrig's eyes were misty as a table full of beautiful gifts was set before him. And tears came to thousands of fans' eyes as Babe Ruth threw his arms around the gallant Gehrig in a huge bear hug. Later Gehrig said to catcher Bill Dickey: "I'll remember this day for a long time."

It was not to be. At the end of the season Gehrig turned in his uniform for good. Less than two years later he was dead, leaving a memory that baseball and Americans would never forget.

By changing the rules, which require a five-year waiting period before a player can be eligible, Gehrig was elected in the Hall immediately after his retirement. His triumphs will always be preserved in the Hall of Fame.

Eddie Collins, second baseman, Philadelphia Athletics/Chicago White Sox, 1906–1930, elected 1939.

Brought up to the big leagues in 1906 at age 19, Collins' 25 years in the majors is a record for modern baseball . . . A sharp fielder and acrobatic pivotman on the double play, Collins was noted more, however, for his effective bat . . . With his shortened, choke grip he hit to all fields . . . Lifetime he was .333 and averaged .340 or better in 10 seasons and attained membership in the exclusive 3000-hit club . . . His 2,825 games is a record for Hall second sackers, as is his 9,949 at bats.

George Sisler, first baseman, St. Louis Browns, 1915–1930, elected 1939.

First basemen are usually rangy guys with a long reach, but George Sisler, at only 5-10½, reached stardom both as fielder and hitter . . . He was nimble around the bag, and seldom dropped a throw, no matter how wild, if he got his glove on it . . . Hit .340, lifetime, and twice had awesome seasons of more than .400 while playing with one of weakest teams in the majors . . . In 1922 he had a 41-game hitting streak that held up as record until Joe DiMaggio broke it in 1941.

Rogers Hornsby, second baseman, St. Louis Cardinals, 1915–1937, elected 1942.

Hornsby was probably the greatest hitter of all time—certainly the greatest righty . . . Because of his bat, fans and experts forgot that he was a flashing, fiery fielder . . . His .424 mark for single season is modern major league record . . . Lifetime mark of .358 is highest ever posted in National League . . . In winning six straight league batting titles, 1921–25, he hit .397, .401, .384, .424, and .403 . . . Pitchers found there wasn't a delivery he couldn't hit—he also poled 302 homers . . . As manager, led Cards to their first World Series crown.

Joe Tinker, shortstop, Chicago Cubs, 1902–1916, elected 1946.

Fans never name one without the other two—Tinker-to-Evers-to-Chance. They were baseball's most famous double-play combination because of their slick artistry and timing when the batted ball went from shortstop-to-second-to-first for two outs . . . They were so good at it that songs and poems were written about them . . . Tinker broke in as a 21 year old with the Cubs and started most of the trio's double plays . . . Five times he led the National League in fielding and was also dangerous at the plate, batting .329 lifetime. Could hit the long ball.

Johnny Evers, second baseman, Chicago Cubs, 1902–1924, elected 1946.

At second base, Evers was more often the pivotman in the Cubs' famed double-play trio . . . A master at timing in either taking the toss from Tinker and firing to first or flipping to Tinker to start the DP . . . Only 140 pounds but never was afraid of flying spikes or being taken out of the play . . . Not known for his hitting but batted a respectable .270 lifetime . . . Fans said he was more second sacker per pound than any man who played the game.

Frank Chance, first baseman, Chicago Cubs, 1898–1914, elected 1946.

The first sacker in the Cubs' famed double-play combo, he naturally was elected to Hall the same year . . . He could handle any kind of throw—high, wide, or in the dirt to end the twin killing . . . A good hitter (.297 lifetime) he was also the Cubs' playing manager and led them to four pennants in five years, and their 116 wins in 1906 were the most ever in big league annals.

Frankie Frisch, second baseman, New York Giants/St. Louis Cardinals, 1919–1937, elected 1947.

Frisch, a star footballer and baseball player at Fordham University, was one of few who went straight from college to big leagues . . . Starting with Giants he went on to glittering 19-year career as player and manager . . . A switch-hitter, he came close to 3,000-hit club with 2,880, and had .300 or better seasons 11 straight years . . . Played on eight pennant winners: three with Giants, five with Cards . . . An intense and sparkling infielder he was hub of defense for both clubs . . . As manager for Cards he led the famed Gas House Gang.

Pie Traynor, third baseman, Pittsburgh Pirates, 1920–1937, elected 1948.

Anyone picking an all-time third baseman could not be criticized for choosing Traynor . . . Quick, sure-handed, and fearless at the "hot corner," where blazing line drives and vicious grounders are common, Traynor could do it all—and was a steady, dependable hitter . . . Not many homers (only 58 career-wise), but he slashed singles and doubles (371) consistently for a lifetime .320 and frequent seasons of 100 RBIs.

Charlie Gehringer, second baseman, Detroit Tigers, 1924–1942, elected 1949.

Without being flashy or dramatic, Gehringer in his 16 years with the Tigers was thought to be the perfect, all-around second sacker . . . A fluid fielder, he never wasted motion even on tough chances . . . Was brilliant double-play artist . . . A smooth-swinging hitter, he batted more than .300 in 13 seasons and one year hit .371 . . . Had a lifetime mark of .320, and though not a power hitter, he had 184 homers and swatted an impressive 575 doubles.

Jimmy Foxx, first baseman, Philadelphia Athletics/Boston Red Sox, 1925–1945, elected 1951.

Foxx was noted not only for his unusual double-x spelling of his name, but for his tremendous hitting power . . . Played three positions—third, catcher, and first, the latter his best post—but it was his home run production which brought him fame . . . Hit 534 homers (7th on all-time list) in a 20-year career; hit 30 or more 12 straight years (big league mark) . . . In 1932 he could have tied Ruth's mark of 60 for a season but lost two homers in games called by rain.

Bill Terry, first baseman, New York Giants, 1923–1936, elected 1954.

A slick-fielding first baseman, Terry gained chief fame as a hitter . . . The crisp-swinging lefty still holds the modern National League career mark for southpaw batters with .341. In nine consecutive years he hit .320 or better . . . Six seasons he ripped out 200 or more hits and was the last National Leaguer to bat .400, with a sensational .401 in 1930 . . . Terry also had great success as a manager, finishing his career as the Giant pilot and winning three NL pennants.

Rabbit Maranville, shortstop, Boston Braves, 1912–1935, elected 1954.

His name was Walter but few people knew that . . . At 5-5, the shortest infielder in the Hall, he was so quick and nimble the nickname had to be his . . . Joined Braves at age 20, played 23 years and 2,670 games, third behind Ty Cobb and Eddie Collins on those lists . . . Only had 28 career homers and .250 lifetime, but was dangerous with men on base . . . His scrappy nature led Braves from last place on July 4, 1914, to first at season's end, with World Series win over favored A's . . . Team gained name Miracle Braves.

Frank Baker, third baseman, Philadelphia Athletics, 1908–1922, elected 1955.

In an era when homers were rare, Baker became known as Home Run Baker because he hit two to win games for the A's in 1911 World Series . . . He had 93 lifetime for 13-year career, with high of 12 in 1913 and led the league four times . . . Baker used an awesome 52-ounce bat but it was the "dead ball" era, and players didn't swing for fences . . . A fancy third baseman, he was part of the best infield in baseball at the time.

Hank Greenberg, first baseman, Detroit Tigers, 1930–1947, elected 1956.

Greenberg, with 58 homers in 1938, fell just two short of Babe Ruth's record . . . The Tigers' big first baseman hit .313 lifetime, and lost four seasons to military service in World War II . . . Overlooked was his brilliant performance in the field, particularly at scooping up throws into the dirt . . . Biggest moment was a grand slam homer to win 1945 AL flag for Detroit . . . Had 331 lifetime homers.

The Major Leagues' First Black Player

Jackie Robinson, second baseman, Brooklyn Dodgers, 1947–1956, elected 1962.

The Brooklyn Dodgers had the bases loaded and the Chicago Cubs' pitcher glanced nervously toward third. Taking a daring lead off third was Jackie Robinson, wearing a confident smile. In the season of

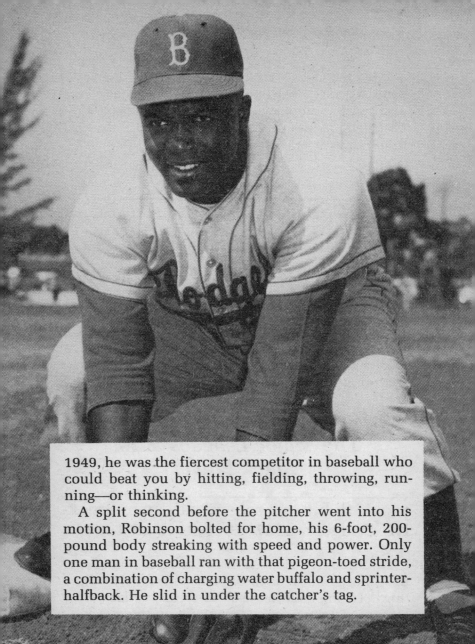

1949, he was the fiercest competitor in baseball who could beat you by hitting, fielding, throwing, running—or thinking.

A split second before the pitcher went into his motion, Robinson bolted for home, his 6-foot, 200-pound body streaking with speed and power. Only one man in baseball ran with that pigeon-toed stride, a combination of charging water buffalo and sprinter-halfback. He slid in under the catcher's tag.

Robinson had stolen home again. He did it 20 times in his career, more than anyone since Ty Cobb. Each time it was a reminder of how dramatic it was that he was in baseball at all.

He would have made the Hall of Fame simply on his abilities but he also belonged because it was Robinson, a black man, who broke the color line and opened the door for future black stars like Roy Campanella, Henry Aaron, Willie Mays, Roberto Clemente, and many others.

Robinson had been one of the greatest college athletes in history, a football-basketball-track star at UCLA. After military service in World War II he played shortstop in 1946 for the Kansas City Monarchs of the Negro Leagues. There he was checked out by Branch Rickey, president of the Dodgers. Rickey thought he had the ability and character to be part of a Great Experiment. Could a black man be accepted in big league baseball?

Rickey sent Robinson to Montreal, then in the International League, but warned him of the problems and racial abuse he would take as the first black man in the pros. Rickey was right. Robinson took tons of abuse from players and fans alike. He could not live in the same hotels as white players. It was agony for a proud athlete like Robinson. But he hung in there.

When Rickey brought him up to the big league Dodgers in training camp in February, 1947, it was just as bad. He had the ability to play anywhere in the infield. April 15, 1947 was a historic date. Jackie Robinson, a black man, was on the field, at first base, for a big league ball club. All that first year he took terrible abuse. Pitchers threw at his head. Some white players said they would boycott any game he appeared in. But the commissioner of baseball said anyone engaging in that boycott would be punished. But the abuse continued. Robinson took it and rebuffed it with his brilliant, slashing style of play. At the end of the year he had everyone's respect—players' and fans' alike. And he was the runaway choice for Rookie-of-the-Year.

In 1949 when he hit .342 to win the league batting crown, he was also the league's MVP. No longer did anyone try to take advantage of him. No longer was he afraid to come sliding into a base with his spikes flashing. He no longer had to hold his tongue when taunts were flung at him. And soon the taunts stopped. Jackie Robinson was just a great baseball player—not just a black player. He retired in 1956 after a glittering 10-year career, with a lifetime batting average of .311 and the reputation as one of the game's great base stealers. And he had proved that black athletes belonged in big league baseball.

Luke Appling, shortstop, Chicago White Sox, 1930–1950, elected 1964.

One of the most difficult men to strike out in big league history . . . His judgment of pitches was legendary . . . Once fouled off ten straight while waiting for one he liked . . . A fine shortstop with a strong arm, he played 20 years with the White Sox, most ever for a shortstop in the American League . . . Hit

.310 for his career and acquired nickname of Old Aches and Pains because he complained so much about injury.

Lou Boudreau, shortstop, Cleveland Indians, 1938–1951, elected 1970.

Although not speedy, Boudreau had uncanny ability to judge hitters and covered tremendous range at short . . . A master at the double play . . . Earlier starred as All-America basketball player at Illinois . . . Fine hitter, had high of .354 one year and a lifetime .295 . . . In 1941, was named manager of the Indians at age 24, second youngest in big league history . . . As player-manager, led Tribe to World Series win over Milwaukee Braves.

Dave Bancroft, shortstop, Philadelphia Phillies/New York Giants, 1915–1930, elected 1971.

At 140 pounds he was one of smallest shortstops ever elected to the Hall of Fame, but he was big in spirit and hustle . . . He hit only 32 homers in his career and his lifetime average of .279 was respectable but not sensational . . . But Bancroft was always up with the leaders in chances, putouts, and assists . . . As a rookie he helped spark the Phillies to their first NL pennant, and when dealt to the Giants in 1920 he was a major force, both at bat and in the field, in the Giants' three straight flags in 1921, '22, and '23.

George Kelly, first baseman, New York Giants, 1915–1932, elected 1973.

At 6-4, Kelly was tallest first baseman ever in NL, and was nicknamed High Pockets for obvious reasons . . . Was a slick, gifted fielder in days when first sackers didn't wear huge, basket-type gloves of today . . . Didn't often hit for distance (only 148 homers) but he used snapping wrist action to give him a lifetime .297 and six straight .300 or over seasons . . . Once got seven homers in six straight games (an NL mark) and still holds NL single-season mark for chances and putouts for first sacker.

Jim Bottomley, first baseman, St. Louis Cardinals, 1922–1937, elected 1974.

A nimble first sacker, he was called Sunny Jim, because he was always smiling and cheerful . . . A star in his own right, he was overshadowed by his Cardinal teammate, superstar Rogers Hornsby, but Bottomley was a consistent hitter, driving in 100 or more runs six straight years . . . Was feared as a dangerous hitter with men on base and seldom struck out with men in scoring position . . . Had a career average of .310 and 219 homers.

Billy Herman, second baseman, Chicago Cubs/Brooklyn Dodgers, 1931–1941, elected 1975.

A fierce competitor, Herman poured all of himself into every play . . . Was the take charge infielder for both the Cubs' and Dodgers' pennant winners in the 1930s and 1940s . . . Among his fielding marks: five seasons of 900 or more chances; led National League second basemen in putouts seven times . . . Not a power hitter but dangerous enough at the plate, with a career mark of .304.

Fred Lindstrom, third baseman, New York Giants, 1924–1936, elected 1976.

In 1924, Lindstrom, at age 18, became youngest man ever to play in World Series . . . Was only a 16-year-old kid when he broke into pro ranks with Toledo Mudhens of the American Association . . . Coming up to the big leagues just two years later, he quickly became one of the game's great fielding third sackers but was also dangerous with his bat . . . Wasn't a noted long-ball hitter but hit .311 lifetime . . . A ground ball hit a pebble in front of him, took a bad hop, and resulted in a Washington Senators' World Series win over the Giants.

Joe Sewell, shortstop, Cleveland Indians, 1920–1933, elected 1977.

Joe Sewell achieved fame not only with his brilliant fielding, but because he was probably the most difficult batter to strike out in the history of big league baseball . . . There would be seasons when Sewell would fan only three or four times the entire campaign . . . He whiffed only 114 times his whole career—14 seasons. (Today, players fan that many times a season.) Batted .312 lifetime . . . Led the league twice in fielding and four times in assists and putouts.

Ernie Banks, shortstop, Chicago Cubs, 1953–1968, elected 1977.

It was Banks' fate that the Cubs were rarely a contender during his 19 years with them, but he was always the bright spot in a mostly dreary situation . . . A fine fielder and smooth on the double play, he was more famed as a hitter . . . Only .274, lifetime, but a long-ball threat with 407 doubles—and one of the game's great home-run hitters with 512 . . . He hit 40 or more in five seasons and one year, 1955, he hit a record five grand slammers.

Eddie Mathews, third baseman, Boston and Milwaukee Braves, 1952–1968, elected 1978.

Mathews was like a vacuum cleaner at third base, stopping anything that came close to him, and had a rifle arm in throwing to first . . . One of the great sluggers of modern times, he had 354 doubles and his 512 homers puts him in the all-time top ten . . . He blasted 40 or more four seasons and 30 or more nine straight seasons . . . In homers among third basemen, is all-time second only to Mike Schmidt of the Phillies.

Johnny Mize, first baseman, St. Louis Cardinals/New York Giants, 1936–1953, elected 1981.

Mize, who batted lefty and threw righty, was an agile first baseman despite his 215-pound bulk, but his career was noted mostly for his hitting . . . In slamming 359 home runs during his career he was the National League leader four times and came close to the title several more times . . . Pitchers feared his power and his mighty swing, and six times he crashed three round-trippers in a single game . . . Although he divided his stardom between Cards and Giants, he wound up playing a few years with the Yankees.

Travis Jackson, shortstop, New York Giants, 1922–1936, elected 1982.

Jackson wasn't very fast, but he had quick reactions, and covered tremendous ground at short ... Because he studied the hitters he was never out of position, and was a sure-handed master of the double play ... For 15 years he had a great batting eye, often drew walks, and hit to all fields ... Finished with a great career mark of .291.

CATCHERS

R oger Bresnahan, catcher, New York Giants, 1897–1915, elected 1945.

Bresnahan was one of the few Hall of Famers who was elected mostly on his sheer ability to play a position, rather than his batting ability . . . Only 5-8, he mastered the art of catching . . . He had great agility and speed—so much speed that he was often used as the Giants' leadoff man in the batting order . . . He was the batterymate of famed super-pitcher Christy Mathewson, and Matty always said Bresnahan was part of his success . . . Bresnahan in 1907 was first catcher to use shin guards.

M ickey Cochrane, catcher, Philadelphia Athletics/Detroit Tigers, 1925–1937, elected 1947.

Cochrane is often called the best all-around catcher the game has produced—but the game almost killed him . . . Beaned while batting in a game in 1937, he hovered between life and death for many days before recovering, and never played again . . . A lifetime .320

hitter, ever dangerous with men on base, he was also a brilliant backstop and handler of pitchers . . . Starred for the A's pennant clubs of 1929, '30, and '31 and then as player-manager for the Tigers, leading them to two flags and a World Series crown.

Bill Dickey, catcher, New York Yankees, 1928–1946, elected 1954.

Tall and storklike, Dickey nevertheless was a smooth and graceful catcher with great throwing arm that discouraged base thefts . . . Few catchers could handle pitchers as well as he did . . . Nearly always knew what pitch to ask for on every batter in league . . . Set a record for receivers by catching 100 or more games per season for 13 straight years . . . One of the game's greatest hitting catchers, he batted .300 or better ten times and slammed 202 homers.

Ray Schalk, catcher, Chicago White Sox, 1912–1929, elected 1955.

Old-timers remember Ray Schalk as the smartest and most agile catcher in the game . . . Weighing only 154, he took pounding at a demanding position but made a science of receiving . . . Was said to be the first catcher to race down to back up plays at first and third—and once was credited with a putout at second . . . He caught 100 games or more for 12 campaigns, including 11 straight seasons . . . Caught four no-hitters, more than any other catcher . . . He only hit 12 homers in his career, but posted respectable .253, lifetime.

Gabby Hartnett, catcher, Chicago Cubs, 1922–1941, elected 1955.

One of the greatest handlers of pitchers the game has known, Hartnett also excelled at nailing base runners on steals, while catching 100 or more games for 12 seasons . . . But he was more visible as a great hitter . . . His career average of .297 was respectable but belied his heavy hitting, which brought him 266 homers and 386 doubles . . . He is third among catchers in all-time homer production . . . Hartnett was also a playing manager for the Cubs, piloting them to a pennant in 1938.

Roy Campanella, catcher, Brooklyn Dodgers, 1948–1957, elected 1969.

When an auto accident left him paralyzed in 1958, ending his fabulous career, Campanella was at his

peak ... The chunky backstop was a brilliant receiver, quick and smart, with a deadly throwing arm, and great savvy in knowing how to pitch to the hitters ... He batted only .276, lifetime, but was a feared long-ball hitter whose 242 homers put him second among catchers only to Yogi Berra of the Yanks.

Yogi Berra, catcher, New York Yankees, 1946–1965, elected 1972.

Berra was an outfielder for a while until he settled in as the Yanks' star catcher . . . Squat and tough at blocking the plate, he also was a smart handler of pitchers . . . But it was Yogi's bat which brought him fame . . . A smooth swinger for a man with short arms and heavy shoulders, he hit .285 lifetime and blasted 358 homers, high among catchers . . . He also played for 14 flag winners and ten World Series champs— a record.

PITCHERS

The First Super Lefty

Christy Mathewson, pitcher, New York Giants, 1900–1916, elected 1936.

There is no pitcher in modern baseball history with a record to match the glittering numbers of Christy Mathewson. He holds the record for most victories in a season, 37.

Four seasons—three of them in a row—he won 30 games or more.

In the 1905 World Series he hurled three straight shutouts.

In 1913 he pitched 68 straight innings without giving up a walk.

He won 373 career games, tying him with Grover Cleveland Alexander in the National League. Cy Young, who won 511 back in the old, *old* days and ended his career in the formal American League, and Walter Johnson, also in the American League, were the only ones to exceed that.

Mathewson was unusual in that he was the first superstar to come from college ranks. At Bucknell University he was not only a great pitcher, but starred in football, was an honor student, president of his class, and a member of the glee club. He could have been a leader in any field he entered. But he loved baseball and had always known that it would be his life.

He had been a pitcher since he was an 11-year-old in Factoryville, Pa. At 14 he was already the star of his town team. One day in nearby Scranton, the pitcher for the local pro team didn't show up. The manager spotted young Christy Mathewson in the stands. He offered the kid two dollars to pitch for him, borrowed a battered extra glove and some spikes, which were too big for him, and sent the kid out to pitch. But first Christy stuffed paper into the huge shoes to make them fit. He then fanned 15 of the opposing pros and won the game.

When he got out of college he joined the Taunton team of the New England League in 1899. After his break-in year, which he always called his "learning year," Mathewson spent a season with Norfolk in the Virginia League. When Norfolk sold his contract to the New York Giants the following season, the big (6-2, 195-pound) righty was on his way to stardom. He won 20 games in his rookie year. Two years later he was a 30-game winner. Then 32. Followed by 31. In three years he had won 93 games!

With the Giants in the 1905 World Series, Mathewson shut out the Philadelphia Athletics with four hits in the first game. The A's won the second game. And when the third game was postponed by rain, Mathewson was able to pitch again with two days' rest. Again he shut out the A's on four hits as the Giants won, 9-0. With the Series shifted to New York, he pitched again—with just one day's rest—and shut out the A's for the third time. The Giants won, 2-0, and took the Series, which was then a best three-of-five affair.

He had a zipping fastball and pinpoint control. He was also among the first to use the so-called fadeaway. When he threw his curve normally, he'd twist his wrist to the right. With his fadeaway he twisted his wrist to the left, so that it broke *toward* right-handed hitters instead of expectedly away from them. It was a devastating delivery. Today it is known as a screwball.

Critics and experts of the day claimed that Mathewson's head was as much responsible for his success as his arm. Highly intelligent, he studied batters as no pitcher had ever done before him. He always recalled what pitches the batters had tagged him for safe hits and rarely threw the same ones to them. He knew how to relax and save his strength for ticklish situations and when he had to be overpowering.

His famous manager, John McGraw, was so impressed by his abilities that Mathewson was the first and only pitcher whom he allowed to call his own pitches. "His judgment is simply better than mine or his catcher's when that ball has to be delivered."

Connie Mack, of the Philadelphia A's, perhaps the most famous and respected manager in baseball history, said: "Christy Mathewson was the greatest pitcher of all time."

He certainly had to be a candidate for that honor. With his 83 career shutouts, 373 victories, .655 winning average, and brilliant 2.13 earned-run average, Christy Mathewson is one of the shiniest stars among the Hall of Fame's greatest.

Presidents Were His Fans

Walter Johnson, pitcher, Washington Senators, 1907–1927, elected 1936.

Walter Johnson, whom many claim was the best pitcher in history, had the misfortune to play with one of the worst teams in the game: the Washington Senators, nearly always in the second division except for a couple of seasons.

But among the exhibits at Cooperstown is a collection of six special baseballs, each with the autograph of a president: Teddy Roosevelt, William Howard Taft, Woodrow Wilson, Warren G. Harding, Calvin Coolidge, and Herbert Hoover. All were fans of Walter Johnson.

Johnson pitched 416 victories, more than any modern American Leaguer in history. He also posted the most shutouts (113), most complete games (532), and most strikeouts (3,499).

The Senators did win two AL pennants, 1924 and '25, but they came at the tail end of Johnson's career, when he was approaching 40. In his 21 years with the club, the Senators played 64 games in which the score was 1-0—indicating how weak their attack was. Yet Johnson won 38 of those games.

Johnson actually started his baseball career as a catcher, a 16-year-old playing with a semipro club in California. He was the catcher because nobody on the team could handle his fastball when he was used as a pitcher.

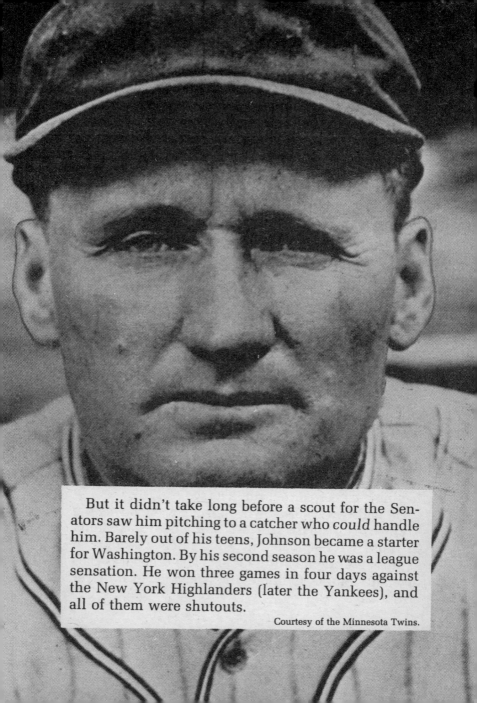

But it didn't take long before a scout for the Senators saw him pitching to a catcher who *could* handle him. Barely out of his teens, Johnson became a starter for Washington. By his second season he was a league sensation. He won three games in four days against the New York Highlanders (later the Yankees), and all of them were shutouts.

By the time he was 22 his fastball was the swiftest in the majors. There are those who said he was the fastest in baseball history, although they didn't have timing machines in those days. He was so strong that he rarely had to rely on a curve. He just blazed the ball past the batters.

Because of his speed he refused to brush back a hitter who crowded the plate, even though his teammates urged him to do so. Just once he relented and whizzed one just inches from the face of the Athletics' Home Run Baker. Baker almost fainted when he realized he nearly was killed. Johnson was just as upset. He never tried to deck another player.

He had 10 straight seasons winning 20 or more games. One year, in 1912, he won 32 games, losing 12. In 1913 his record was 36–7. Eleven times he led the AL in strikeouts. Despite his fastball, he never had arm trouble and never complained about the overall weakness of the Senators. He just went out there and pitched. Against great odds, knowing his club would get him very few runs, he won 16 straight games one season. He had other streaks of 10, 11, and 14. The kid of 20 who'd won three games in four days was the same man who won 20 games at age 38. Can you imagine a pitcher, after a 21-year career, having a career earned-run average of 2.17?

He had two well-known nicknames. One was Big Train, because of his size (6-1, 200, which was a hunk in those days) and because his pitch was like an express roaring down the track. The other was Barney, after Barney Oldfield, the famed race-car driver of the day.

Throughout his career he was known as one of the premier gentlemen in the game, whom everyone liked and respected. That is why six presidents of the United States autographed baseballs for him.

Cy Young, pitcher, Cleveland Indians, 1890–1911, elected 1937.

Voted into the Hall in its second election, he is the man after whom the Cy Young Award is named. It is given every year to the outstanding pitchers in each of the two major leagues ... For good reason the honor is named for him. His skill and durability went hand in hand ... His 511 victories far outdistance any other hurler by almost 100 ... He was a 20 game or more winner for 16 seasons, and 14 of those years were consecutive ... In his 22-year career, he won more than 30 games five times, and in 1904 he performed the incredible feat of pitching a perfect, 24-inning game against Philadelphia A's, one of three no-hitters he had. In all, he worked 906 games, set the all-time mark for innings pitched with 7,377, and had a career earned-run mark of only 2.63.

Grover Cleveland Alexander, pitcher, St. Louis Cardinals, 1911–1930, elected 1938.

One of the most colorful pitchers in big league history and the only one named after a president

(Grover Cleveland), Old Alex worked amazing feats in his 20 seasons . . . With good speed, baffling curves, and superb control he pitched 696 games, fourth highest of all pitchers; had 90 shutouts, second only to Walter Johnson's record 113; had a 373–209 record for a shining .642 and a sparkling ERA of 2.56 . . . His 373 wins tied him with the legendary Christy Mathewson for tops in the National League . . . In 1915 he pitched four one-hitters, and the following year he had 16 shutouts, a big league record . . . In the 1926 World Series he wasn't expected to pitch in the 7th game of the Series and had been out partying the night before . . . Called to the mound in the 7th inning with bases loaded, Alexander fanned Yankee slugger Tony Lazzeri to win the Series for the Cardinals . . . In the twilight of his career, despite all his previous feats, it was his shiniest moment in the minds of his fans.

Eddie Plank, pitcher, Philadelphia Athletics, 1901–1917, elected 1946.

Going straight from Gettysburg College to the A's, Plank worked 17 years with the Athletics, earning fame as one of the game's greatest lefties . . . His 326 wins are second only to the modern ace Warren Spahn among lefties all-time . . . His 69 shutouts are high for any left-hander, and rarely did he have to give way to relief pitcher . . . Eight seasons he won 20 or more contests and helped lead drive to six pennants for the Athletics.

Ed Walsh, pitcher, Chicago White Sox, 1904–1917, elected 1946.

Incredible durability and strength marked Ed Walsh, who twice won two games in a single day (double-headers). Once, in 1908, he allowed only one run in the twin bill . . . Averaging 25 wins a season in a six-year period with the White Sox, he set a modern mark in pitching 464 innings in 1908. Won 40 games that year . . . His earned-run-average of 1.82 career-wise, is the all-time big league record for giving up fewest runs.

Rube Waddell, pitcher, Philadelphia Athletics / St. Louis Browns, 1897–1910, elected 1946.

Rube Waddell, who was never much for training rules or discipline, was all seriousness when he took the mound . . . Veteran manager Connie Mack claimed Waddell was the best lefty he'd ever seen . . . A fire-baller, he had more than 2,300 strikeouts in his career, and in his 191 career wins he had an amazing 50 shutouts, a very high percentage . . . Led league in strikeouts six straight seasons . . . Led the A's to two pennants and had sensational earned-run mark of 2.16 . . . Ended career with Browns and once fanned 16 in a game, then a record.

Carl Hubbell, pitcher, New York Giants, 1928–1943, elected 1947.

They didn't call him King Carl or The Meal Ticket for nothing . . . The slender left-handed hurler paced the Giants to pennants in 1933, '36, and '37, with a World Series win in 1933 . . . With fine control and wide assortment of pitches, he once went 46 straight scoreless innings and won 16 straight in 1936 . . . In his most dramatic performance, the 1934 All-Star game, he whiffed Babe Ruth, Lou Gehrig, Jimmie Foxx, Al Simmons, and Joe Cronin in a row—all Famers.

Lefty Grove, Philadelphia Athletics/Boston Red Sox, 1925–1941, elected 1947.

The lanky lefty led the red-hot Philadelphia A's to pennants in 1929, '30, and '31, with World Series crowns in 1929 and '30 . . . His presence helped make the A's one of the greatest clubs of all time . . . A 300-game winner lifetime, he had eight 20 or more years . . . For seven straight years he led the league in strike-outs, and in 1931 he had a sensational 31–4 record . . . Possibly the finest lefty in AL history, he had a super .680 average on a 300–141 record.

Herb Pennock, pitcher, Philadelphia Athletics/Boston Red Sox/New York Yankees, 1912–1934, elected 1948.

Pennock had one of the longest pitching careers in the majors—22 seasons . . . Went to the A's right from high school and three years later to the Red Sox . . . After a few seasons he was traded to the Yanks where he established himself as a real star . . . The slim lefty worked 617 games in his career and his 240–162 record left him just short of the heralded .600 mark at .597 . . . A World Series ace, he won five for the Yanks.

Mordecai Brown, pitcher, Chicago Cubs, 1903–1915, elected 1949.

Among old-time hurlers, Brown is most often compared to the legendary Christy Mathewson as the National League's greatest pitcher . . . In leading the Cubs in their dynasty days, he won 20 or more games six straight seasons as the Cubs won pennants in 1906, '07, '08, and '10 . . . All this despite having lost parts of two fingers on his pitching hand, in a farm accident as a boy . . . He had an impressive 2.03 ERA.

Chief Bender, pitcher, Philadelphia Athletics, 1903–1925, elected 1953.

Nobody knew if he had another name. He was simply Chief, because he was a full-blooded Indian who'd been a football and baseball star at Carlisle Indian School in Pennsylvania . . . After finishing his education in 1902 at age 19, he was signed by the A's and became an instant star . . . The big (6-2), dark-eyed Minnesota Indian sparked the A's to five AL pennants and two World Series triumphs . . . Led league in won-lost percentage three times.

Jay (Dizzy) Dean, pitcher, St. Louis Cardinals, 1930–1947, elected 1953.

One of the most colorful pitchers in history, the blazing righty feared no hitter and bragged of his feats, but always said: "If you done it, it ain't braggin'." . . . Had amazing confidence along with his poise . . . In his first five years with the Cards he averaged 24 wins a season, led the league in strike-outs four times, and had a high of 30–7 in 1934, the year he and brother Paul (Daffy) won World Series against Detroit with all four victories between them . . . Arm trouble from an injury in 1937 All-Star game shortened his career at 150-83—a fine .644 average.

Dazzy Vance, pitcher, Brooklyn Dodgers, 1915–1935, elected 1955.

Vance reached the majors at an older age (31) than anyone in the Hall . . . He toiled almost 10 years in the minors with a sore arm, but when he came up to the big leagues he became the Brooklyn Dodgers most famous pitcher—and possibly their best, all-time . . . In 14 seasons (he pitched until he was in his mid-forties), he won 197 games . . . His blazing fastball enabled him to lead the National League in strikeouts seven straight years . . . In 1924 he won 15 in a row.

Ted Lyons, pitcher, Chicago White Sox, 1923–1944, elected 1955.

Known for control and mastery of many different pitches, Lyons was one of the truly fine mound stars of the 1920s and 1930s . . . Pitched 21 years for the White Sox, a league mark for pitching service with one club . . . He won 260 for a team rarely finishing in the first division, yet put out 110% every time he started—and in fact finished a higher percentage of his games than most hurlers on championship clubs.

Eppa Rixey, pitcher, Philadelphia Phillies/Cincinnati Reds, 1912–1933, elected 1963.

Among things Rixey is noted for: He is the only man in all baseball with the given name, Eppa, and at 6-5½ he is the tallest player in the Hall . . . Just as notably, he was one fine pitcher, and until Warren Spahn of recent fame, was the third winningest (266) pitcher in the National League, after Mathewson and Alexander . . . Rixey started winning right out of college (Virginia) and kept winning (266–251) even though his clubs rarely got out of the second division . . . Pitched 21 years and once in 1922 led the NL with 25 victories.

Bob Feller, pitcher, Cleveland Indians, 1936–1956, elected 1962.

As 18-year-old rookie, the big right-hander struck out 17 batters in a single game and went on to fastball stardom . . . By age 20 was a 24-game winner . . . As a 13-year-old farm boy from Iowa, he first threw to his father behind their barn and big league scouts came running . . . Had three no-hitters and a record 12 one-hitters in his career . . . Four years in military service during World War II kept him from becoming a 300-game winner . . . Came back from the war and regained his magic touch . . . In first year back (1946) he fanned 348 . . . Won 266 games.

Burleigh Grimes, pitcher, St. Louis Cardinals/Chicago Cubs/New York Giants, 1916–1934, elected 1964.

Chunky Burleigh Grimes toiled 19 years for seven different big league clubs, but did his most effective work for the Cards, Cubs, and Giants . . . He won 270 games, relying on speed, control, and a spitter . . . Was last of the legal NL spitballers before the pitch was banned . . . Five times won 20 or more games and was a big cog in the Cardinals' pennant drives of 1930 and '31 and the Cubs' flag winner of 1932.

Charles H. (Red) Ruffing, pitcher, New York Yankees, 1924–1947, elected 1967.

Ruffing was the cool, masterful artist with brilliance on every delivery: fastball, curve, slider, change-up. Had great control while winning 273 games . . . As a youth, played in outfield but lost several toes in mining accident where he worked, and wasn't fast enough for outfield after that . . . Switched to pitching as a pro and made his mark with four straight 20 game or better years . . . At his best in World Series play, winning seven of nine starts with the Yanks.

Waite Hoyt, pitcher, New York Giants/Boston Red Sox/New York Yankees/Pittsburgh Pirates/Brooklyn Dodgers, 1918–1938, elected 1969.

His earned-run average of 3.59 is not one of the better ones in the Hall, but Hoyt was very consistent and had a knack of pitching himself out of bad spots . . . Although signed at age 15 by the Giants, he was traded to the Yanks soon after coming up to the majors and was effective for 21 seasons ... He worked three complete World Series games in 1921 against his old team, the Giants, and allowed only two runs—both unearned ... He was a Yankee star in six of their pennant-winning seasons.

Urban (Red) Faber, pitcher, Chicago White Sox, 1914–1923, elected 1964.

Fans often wondered what Red Faber could have done with a pennant contender instead of the lowly White Sox, who never were out of second division in 15 of 20 years Faber pitched for them ... Strong and mentally tough, he even won 25 games in 1921 when Sox finished seventh and had a brilliant earned-run mark of 2.47 that year ... In lone pennant year of his career with Sox he beat the Giants three times in World Series ... Was last legal spitballer in AL.

Stan Coveleski, pitcher, Cleveland Indians, 1912–1928, elected 1969.

Coveleski was one of few pitchers ever to win three victories in one World Series, starring for Cleveland against Brooklyn Dodgers in 1920, granting Dodgers a total of two runs ... Won 20 or more in five seasons and one year had string of 13 straight ... Only 5-9½, he had great stamina, determination, and

concentration and posted 216 wins lifetime . . . Had an outstanding .650 percentage on 327–167 and an earned-run average of only 2.87 . . . Credited his great control to throwing rocks at tin cans as a boy.

Jesse Haines, pitcher, St. Louis Cardinals, 1918–1937, elected 1970.

Never a superstar but always a shining light, Haines is an honored member of the 200-Win Club, with 210 . . . The right-hander appeared in 555 games in his service with the Cards, had three 20-game seasons, and was a big winner in years when the Cards were a second division club . . . A canny vet who mastered many of the great hitters of his day, he beat the Yankees twice in the 1926 World Series.

Rube Marquard, pitcher, New York Giants, 1908–1922, elected 1971.

Marquard was one of the pitching sensations of the early 1900s, succeeding the great Christy Mathewson as the pride of New York . . . Led by the tall (6-3½) Rube, the Giants won three straight NL flags (1911, '12, and '13) losing three times to the A's in the World Series . . . Marquard won 72 games in that stretch—a brilliant feat—and had everyone talking in 1912 when he won 19 straight . . . He spent his last few seasons with Brooklyn Dodgers and led them to their first NL flag in 1916.

Leroy (Satchel) Paige, pitcher, Cleveland Indians and several other teams, 1948–1965, elected 1971.

Leroy (Satchel) Paige was said to have pitched 2,500 games and won 2,000 of them in the Negro Leagues before getting a chance in the majors as a 42-year-old rookie (he was probably older) . . . Said to have had 100 no-hitters in the Negro Leagues, he still had a blazing fastball and wicked curve in the big leagues . . . Was a winning pitcher in the six seasons he played on-and-off in the majors over many in-and-out years. Pitched his last game at age 59 and still had great stuff.

Earl Wynn, pitcher, Washington Senators/Cleveland Indians/Chicago White Sox, 1939–1963, elected 1972.

Wynn made the magic circle of 300 pitching wins with an even 300, and did it over 23 seasons—longest career of any major league hurler . . . Forty-five were shutouts . . . With strength and good stuff, Wynn was a 20-game winner five times and was a big cog in the Cleveland Indians' pennant of 1954, and again in 1959 when he led the White Sox to the flag . . . That year he won the Cy Young Award at age 39, oldest pitcher to win it.

The Modern Game's Greatest Southpaw

Sandy Koufax, pitcher, Brooklyn and Los Angeles Dodgers, 1955–1966, elected 1972.

As a boy in Brooklyn, Sanford (Sandy) Koufax was crazy about basketball. He played some baseball, too, but it was basketball that was his real love, and he won a scholarship to the University of Cincinnati. He played basketball there for two years, but something happened on what he thought would be his way to the NBA. Something told him that it was baseball he loved most, and having played a season for the Bearcats he decided that's where his sports future would take him.

With the Los Angeles Dodgers, it took him a long way.

Now, on the night of September 9, 1965, Sandy Koufax was warming up, his mind on the Chicago Cubs' batters he'd face. Who to use the sharp curve on, who the slider, who the fastball.

Just four days earlier, for about the 29th time that year, he had to sit for a half-hour after the game with his left arm packed in ice. He'd developed a blood circulation problem in 1962 and later there was painful arthritis in his pitching elbow.

Tonight he was feeling good. The Dodgers were only a half-game behind the league-leading Giants. Every game would be a big one from now on. Es-

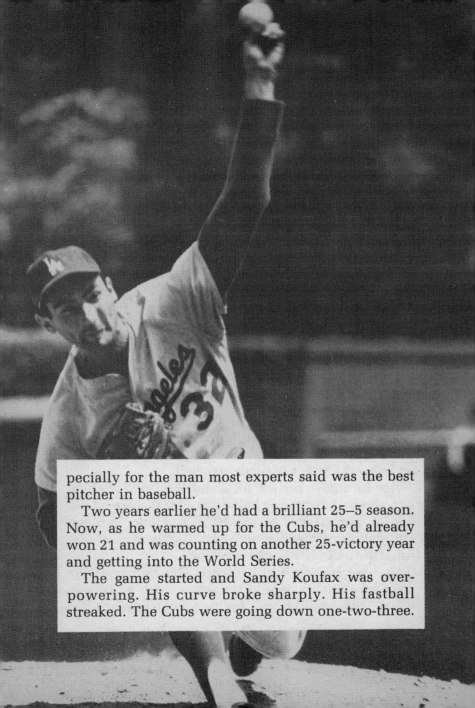

pecially for the man most experts said was the best pitcher in baseball.

Two years earlier he'd had a brilliant 25–5 season. Now, as he warmed up for the Cubs, he'd already won 21 and was counting on another 25-victory year and getting into the World Series.

The game started and Sandy Koufax was overpowering. His curve broke sharply. His fastball streaked. The Cubs were going down one-two-three.

The Dodgers got an unearned run in the sixth, but the Cubs had yet to get a hit. The Dodgers had only one hit themselves. It was an epic pitchers' battle between Koufax and Bob Hendley.

By the eighth inning there was only one thought among the 30,000 fans. Could Koufax hold onto his no-hitter? Also his perfect game, because no Cub had reached first? Now, in the eighth, Koufax faced Ron Santo, Ernie Banks, and Byron Browne. Three tough ones. He fanned all three.

First up for the Cubs in the ninth was Chris Krug. His throwing error had allowed the Dodgers their lone run. He was determined to make up for it. Koufax fanned him.

Pinch hitter Joe Amalfitano came to the plate. The tension in the air fairly sizzled. Players were tight-lipped. Fans almost held their breath. Koufax struck out Amalfitano, swinging.

Up came Harvey Kuenn, a one-time American League batting champ, now with the Cubs. Kuenn went down swinging. And with the swish of his bat came the roaring sound from the stands.

Sandy Koufax had pitched his no-hit, perfect game.

He had also become the first man in big league history to pitch four no-hitters. On June 30, 1962, Koufax got his first one, beating the Mets, 5-0. On May 11, 1963 he got his second, 8-0, over the Giants. His third was on June 4, 1964, beating the Phillies, 3-0. Now, on September 9, 1965 he had set down the Cubs. A no-hitter every year for four straight years!

The Dodgers went on to win the NL crown and beat Minnesota in the World Series, 4–3, with Koufax losing once and beating Minnesota twice. He was 26–

8 that year. The following season it looked as though he'd be the first 30-game winner since Lefty Grove. But his left arm wouldn't cooperate. The arthritic pain was too much. He settled for 27–9. Not exactly shabby.

Sandy Koufax was forced to retire after the 1966 season. There wasn't a fan or baseball player in the big leagues who wouldn't have bet he'd get his fifth and even a sixth no-hitter over the next couple seasons.

His mark of four, just one behind Nolan Ryan, is evidence enough of his lasting greatness. Baseball's Hall of Fame helps insure that.

Lefty Gomez, pitcher, New York Yankees, 1930–1948, elected 1972.

His teammates called him Goofy Gomez because he was always wisecracking and displaying a great sense of humor . . . But opposing batters found him anything but funny . . . Not an overpowering pitcher, but a crafty one with good fastball and wicked curve . . . Four times a 20-game winner, the tall lefty was stingy with hits allowed . . . Twice led the American League in won-loss percentage and three times in strikeouts . . . Holds World Series record of six wins without loss and helped Yankees to seven AL pennants.

War Hero Returned to Stardom

Warren Spahn, pitcher, Boston and Milwaukee Braves, 1942–1965, elected 1973.

If it hadn't been for World War II, Warren Spahn probably would have won more games than any player in modern history. Even so, he almost wasn't a pitcher. In Buffalo, N.Y., his father spent days on end teaching him to pitch, but Warren's high school coach played him in the outfield where he was such a tremendous hitter he made the All-City team.

But in his senior year his coach no longer could deny the boy's demands to pitch and let him take the mound. That is where the then-Boston Braves saw him and signed him for one of their farm teams. Their instructions to the boy's manager was to find out whether he was an outfielder, first baseman, or pitcher. They invested an $80-a-month salary in him to find out.

He advanced up through the minors, looking good on the mound. Just when the Braves decided he was worth a shot in the big leagues, Spahn was drafted into the army. Sent to Europe, the young pitching hopeful was content to just stay alive. He saw bitter fighting in France and Germany, and his outfit was the first American unit to cross the Rhine River in pursuit of the Germans. For bravery under fire he won a battlefield commission from sergeant to lieutenant, right on the spot.

Rejoining the Braves in 1946 it took him a year to get used to the relative peace of baseball, but by 1947

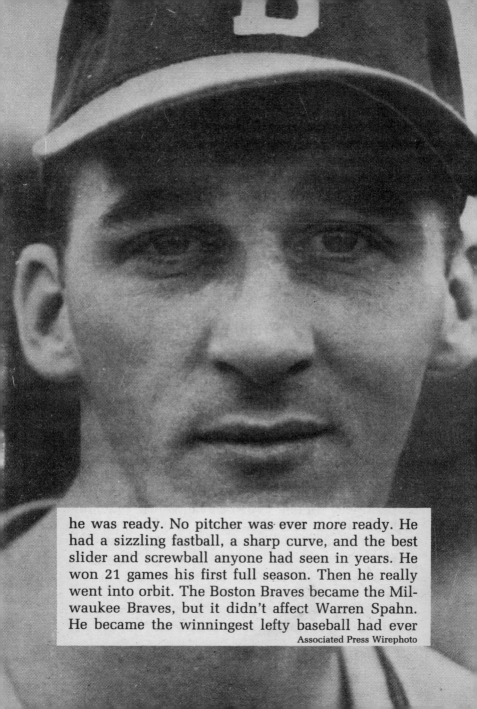

he was ready. No pitcher was ever more ready. He had a sizzling fastball, a sharp curve, and the best slider and screwball anyone had seen in years. He won 21 games his first full season. Then he really went into orbit. The Boston Braves became the Milwaukee Braves, but it didn't affect Warren Spahn. He became the winningest lefty baseball had ever known, winning 363 games. In 13 seasons he won 20 or more games, six of those years in a row.

In his 20-year career he pitched 63 shutouts. He set big league marks for most seasons of 20 or more wins with seven; for most years leading in games won, eight; most consecutive years leading in complete games, seven; most strikeouts by a lefty, 2,583; most consecutive years with 100 or more strikeouts, 17. And his 750 games started were the most by any NL pitcher. What more could you want for a Hall of Famer? The Braves will always remember him because in 1948 he led them to their first NL pennant in 35 years.

Johnny Sain, his pitching buddy with the Braves, practically worshiped Spahn. "He was the complete pitcher and ball player," said Sain. "He was the best-hitting pitcher in the league. He could run the bases. He was a great fielder off the mound. He had a terrific pickoff move to first. He was the only pitcher alive who ever picked Jackie Robinson off first—twice in one game.

"He also had a memory like an elephant," Sain continued. "One of the league's best hitters once got a double off a fastball Spahn had thrown him high and inside. The guy didn't see a fastball, high and inside, off Spahn for the next 10 years."

So durable was Warren Spahn that he didn't get his first no-hitter until he was 39 years old, long after most pitchers are retired. He used only 105 pitches in the game—remarkably low. One year later, just after his 40th birthday, Warren Spahn got his second no-hitter, and also won 21 games that season.

National League hitters feared he'd stick around until he was 50. But he'd done all he'd wanted to and retired at age 44.

Whitey Ford, pitcher, New York Yankees, 1950–1967, elected 1974.

When the Yankees were destroying the AL and piling up World Series wins in the 1950s and 1960s, Ford was one of the big reasons . . . A crafty lefty with a bewildering assortment of pitches, Ford's 236–106 career mark gives him a .690 percentage, highest of any modern hurler . . . Three times he led the league in wins and twice in shutouts and earned-run average . . . His 10 World Series victories and 94 strike-outs are records.

Robin Roberts, pitcher, Philadelphia Phillies, 1948–1966, elected 1976.

If Roberts had been with a constant flag contender he probably would have been recognized as one of the all-time greats, but the Phillies were mostly in the second division during his lengthy 19-year career with them . . . But his great range of pitches and fine control produced six 20-game years for the Michigan Stater and in 1950 he was the leader of the Phillies' drive to their first NL flag in 35 seasons.

Bob Lemon, pitcher, Cleveland Indians, 1946–1958, elected 1976.

Lemon is another case of a minor leaguer who came out of the infield or outfield to achieve stardom as a big league pitcher . . . More recently known as manager of the Yankees, he was a superstar for the Indians, winning 20 games or more seven times in a nine-year period, leading the Tribe to American League pennants in 1948 and 1954 . . . A lifetime winning percentage of .600 or better is a bright plateau for pitchers, and Lemon reached .618.

Addie Joss, pitcher, Cleveland Blues and Cleveland Naps, 1902–1910, elected 1978.

How'd you like to have a pitcher on your staff with a lifetime earned-run average of 1.88? That's how amazingly effective Joss was in posting the second lowest ERA in big league history . . . The lanky (6-3) right-hander mowed 'em down with a big curve and great control . . . Winning more than 20 games a season, four straight years, Joss's career was cut short at age 31 by serious illness . . . His 45 shutouts in 160 career wins is the highest percentage in the Hall.

Bob Gibson, pitcher, St. Louis Cardinals, 1955–1968, elected 1981.

Gibson was easily one of most gifted, all-around pitchers the game has known . . . With a blazing fastball, tricky change-of-pace, and great control, he won 251 in his 17-year career and reached the 3,000 strikeout level (3,117) rarely reached by pitchers . . . Perhaps more important, his brilliant 2.91 earned-run average put him under the 3.0 mark . . . He won two Cy Young awards as pitcher of the year and won seven straight World Series games for Cards.

THE <u>OLD</u> OLD-TIMERS

Professional baseball flourished many years before the formal organization of the National and American Leagues in the early 1900s. There were many teams in the top-ranked leagues in the 1880s and 1890s. Stars of that era are recognized in Baseball's Hall of Fame. In many cases, the years of their performance are obscure, and they are merely listed as 19th century.

Harry Wright, outfielder, Cincinnati Redlegs/Boston Red Stockings, 19th century, elected 1937.

It was Harry Wright who organized the Cincinnati Redlegs, baseball's first pro club, and was dubbed Father of Professional Baseball . . . He also played the outfield as the Red Stockings won all their 69 contests . . . He was also the originator of knicker trousers—the first uniform . . . Later he managed the Boston Red Stockings to a half-dozen league flags and guided baseball's first foreign tour, to England in 1876.

George Wright, shortstop, Cincinnati Redlegs/Boston Red Stockings, 19th century, elected 1937.

It was only fitting that Wright should have made the Hall because he was the star of baseball's first pro club, the Cincinnati Redlegs, in a day when 500 fans was a good crowd at a game . . . The Redlegs, organized in 1869, had Wright at shortstop where he made brilliant plays and hit 49 homers in a 56-game schedule . . . Later he starred for the Boston Red Stockings, pacing them to four straight league titles and hit more than .325 each year . . . He pioneered the art of playing shortstop well behind the base line.

Cap Anson, first baseman and manager, Chicago White Sox, 1876–1897, elected 1939.

Cap Anson, first legendary star of early pro baseball, was the first player to record 3,000 hits . . . He had a dual reputation as the game's first great slugger and as a successful manager of the White Sox . . . In 22 seasons he failed to hit .300 only twice, and twice hit more than .400 . . . Still an active player at 45, he hit .303 that year and finished .339 lifetime.

Charles (Old Hoss) Radbourne, pitcher, Providence Grays, 19th century, elected 1939.

Another star born before the Civil War, Radbourne had one of baseball's first nicknames (Old Hoss) because of his steadiness and durability . . . In the 1884 season he worked the Grays' last 27 games—and won 26 of them . . . Pitching only 11 seasons, he won an amazing 308 games . . . In that 1884 campaign he had a 60–12 record.

Charles Comiskey, first baseman, Chicago White Stockings, 19th & 20th centuries, elected 1939.

Although Charley Comiskey was noted as owner of the White Sox far into the modern part of the 20th century, he had won earlier fame as a player . . . Although just a fair hitter, he was dependable with runners on base and was said to have invented the style for first baseman to play several feet off the bag . . . After his playing days he was one of the two men who led in the formation of the modern American League.

Candy Cummings, pitcher, New York Mutuals, 19th century, elected 1939.

Cummings deserves special mention among Famers if only for one reason: He was said to be the first to experiment with the curveball . . . Many pitchers had still been throwing the ball underhanded, but when Cummings went to overhanded delivery, the curve was his big contribution to the game . . . In his first year with the New York Mutuals of the National Association he won 34, lost 19.

Buck Ewing, catcher/outfield/infield, several teams, 19th century, elected 1939.

Old-timers said Ewing was the most versatile of the 19th-century pros, playing catcher, outfield, and infield positions with equal and great ability . . . As a catcher and outfielder he was noted for a powerful arm, but he was also a brilliant hitter, batting .300 or more in 11 of his big league years, including 66 homers, a highly productive mark for the dead ball era.

Mike (King) Kelly, Chicago White Stockings/Boston Beaneaters, 19th century, elected 1945.

The baseball cry of "Slide, Kelly, Slide!" was the most famous chant of fans in the 19th century . . .

King Kelly with the Chicago White Stockings was the most daring base runner of the day . . . But his fans cheered him as a hitter, too, as he led his team to five championships in the 1880s . . . He was also said to be the inventor of the hit-and-run play . . . Later he starred for the Boston Beaneaters.

Jim O'Rourke, outfielder, Boston/Providence, 19th century, elected 1945.

O'Rourke was one of the earliest pro stars, after joining the Boston Red Stockings as an outfielder fresh out of Yale Law School . . . Combining two careers, he led the Red Stockings to five championships with his slashing hits, gaining a lifetime average of .314 . . . It was said that he played pro ball until he was 50, and then became an umpire and manager.

Jimmy Collins, third baseman, several Massachusetts teams, 19th century, elected 1945.

Collins was considered the best all-around third sacker before the turn of the century . . . Sure-handed at the hot corner, he was a defensive whiz and was called the "hit robber" by his foes . . . The little (5-8) Collins was a giant at bat, and with men on base was one of the most feared batters of his era.

Fred Clarke, outfielder, Louisville Colonels/Pittsburgh Pirates, 19th century, elected 1945.

Clarke was an early player-manager, starring for the Louisville Colonels . . . He broke in as a rookie in the early 1890s by going five-for-five and as a vet hit .406, while managing . . . When the Colonels merged with Pittsburgh at the turn of the century, he piloted the Pirates to three straight pennants and a World Series win in 1909.

Dan Brouthers, first baseman, Detroit Wolverines, 19th century, elected 1945.

Another heavy hitter who pulverized the so-called dead ball of the 19th century was Brouthers, an early Detroit Wolverine first baseman who hit .300 or better 14 straight seasons and captured five major league batting crowns . . . One year he hit .419 (in an era when a walk was counted as a hit) but lost the batting championship to Cap Anson by two points.

Ed Delahanty, outfielder, Philadelphia/Washington, 19th century, elected 1945.

Easily top-ranked among the old-time superstars, Delahanty's heroics were mostly as a batter in the days of the so-called dead ball . . . His lifetime average of .346 is fourth best of all-time big leaguers and he alone won batting crowns in two leagues . . . Twice he was six-for-six in a single game, and once was nine-for-nine in a doubleheader . . . Twice he hit .400 . . . He was one of five brothers who played in the majors.

Jack Chesbro, pitcher, Pittsburgh Pirates/ New York Highlanders, 19th century, elected 1946.

Chesbro broke in with the Pirates and led them to an NL pennant but won most of his fame when he went to the New York Highlanders of the AL (fore-runner of the Yankees) . . . Only 5-9, he astounded fans and overwhelmed hitters in 1904 when he was the starter in 51 games, finishing 48, and winning 41 of them . . . In five years, 1901–1906, he won 154 games, averaging better than 25 wins a season . . . With ERA of 2.68, was one of few hurlers to lead both majors in won-lost percentage.

Jesse Burkett, outfielder, Cleveland Spi-ders/St. Louis Cardinals, 19th century, elected 1946.

A solid, alert outfielder in the days of the early major leagues, Burkett was one of the batting stars of his day . . . Three times he hit .400 or better for the season, one of only three players ever to do so (plus Ty Cobb and Rogers Hornsby) . . . In his 15-year career he led the then NL in hitting three times . . . He only hit 70 homers (pretty good for his era) but compiled an impressive lifetime batting mark of .342.

Sam Thompson, outfielder, Detroit Wolverines/Philadelphia Phillies, 1883–1906, elected 1974.

Thompson was one of the big rifle-arms of the early major leagues, and few base runners took liberties with him . . . He was also a famed hitter, particularly with men on base . . . He batted .336 lifetime and was feared as a home-run hitter before the turn of the century. Had 128 in his career . . . Twice he hit .400 or better for the season, and three times marked up the magic number of 200 or more hits in a season.

Joe McGinnity, pitcher, New York Giants, 19th century, elected 1946.

There were two reasons why Joe McGinnity was called Iron Man . . . He worked in a foundry, and he was possibly the most durable pitcher at the turn of the century . . . On his way to a dandy .630 lifetime percentage, he often (five times) worked both ends

of doubleheaders, three times winning both games . . .
Tough and husky, McGinnity thought nothing of
pitching 400 or more innings per season and set a
record of 434 in 1903, which still stands as a National
League mark.

Tom McCarthy, outfielder, several teams, 19th century, elected 1946.

McCarthy was a versatile player who could hit,
field, and run bases and often was in the headlines
of early sports pages of the late 19th century . . . In
1888, as the St. Louis Browns won their first and
only pennant until 1944, he stole 109 bases and was
their star outfielder and timely hitter . . . Later he
starred as an outfielder for the Boston Beaneaters for
several seasons.

Kid Nichols, pitcher, Boston Beaneaters, 19th century, elected 1949.

Charles A. (Kid) Nichols was another old-timer who
starred before the eventual formation of the two modern major leagues . . . He got his nickname because
he was only 20 when he joined the AL Beaneaters . . .
In the loosely organized competition of the late 19th
century he won 20 or more for 10 years, and in seven
of them won 30 or more . . . He had 27 wins in his
rookie year and was known for his wicked curve.

Bobby Wallace, shortstop, St. Louis Browns, 19th century, elected 1953.

Bobby Wallace was another of those pint-sized shortstops (5-8) who specialized in robbing batters of base hits . . . For years he was the spark of the Browns' infield and three times led the American League in fielding percentage and assists . . . In 1902 he set an all-time AL record of successfully handling 17 chances in one game without an error . . . When his playing days were over he became an umpire.

John Ward, shortstop, New York Giants, 19th century, elected 1964.

Ward, one of 13 old-time players who was born before the Civil War (1860), starred in the early days of organized pro leagues . . . When an arm injury put a halt to his pitching career in Providence he went to the New York Giants as a shortstop, where he dazzled in the field as the Giants won NL flags in 1888–1889 . . . He hit a respectable .283, lifetime . . . Late in his career he was a playing manager for the New Yorkers.

Tim Keefe, pitcher, several teams, 19th century, elected 1964.

Fireplug-sized Tim Keefe, another star born before the Civil War, sparkled for several pro clubs in the

1870s and 1880s as a pitcher . . . Winning 344 games in 14 years, he was a 40-game winner twice and was said to be one of the earlier masters of change of pace strategy . . . In one season, 1888, he won 19 straight.

Pud Galvin, pitcher, several clubs, 19th century, elected 1965.

Born in 1855, before the Civil War began, Galvin broke into pro ball in his late teens and became baseball's first 300-game winner (361) and in his day was the iron man of the game, twice pitching more than 70 complete games . . . In his career he completed more games (649) than anyone in baseball except the immortal Cy Young, after whom the pitching award is named . . . He was also considered a threat with his bat.

Jake Beckley, first baseman, 19th century, elected 1971.

Beckley, a classy fielder at first base, gained most of his fame with his bat, hitting .300 or more 13 seasons . . . His lifetime 2,930 hits left him a bit short of the prized plateau of 3,000. He batted .309 in his career, with long-ball stats of 455 doubles and 246 triples . . . He also set big league standards for put-outs and chances at first base.

Joe Kelley, outfielder, Baltimore Orioles/ New York Superbas, 19th century, elected 1971.

The old Baltimore Orioles, one of the greatest of the early pro clubs, had many stars, but few brighter than Kelley . . . Kelley was not only a swift, sparkling fielder with a strong arm but was a fine hitter . . . Eleven straight years he batted .300 or more and could hit the long ball, with 66 homers, 183 triples, and 358 doubles . . . He once was nine-for-nine in a doubleheader.

Mickey Welch, pitcher, Troy Trojans/New York Gothams/New York Giants, 19th century, elected 1973.

In the old days, pitchers weren't pampered . . . When in trouble they had to pitch out of it with little relief . . . Welch was amazing in that respect, pitching full games in his first 105 starts—and once won both ends of a doubleheader . . . Just missing the shining plateau of a .600 average with his career .596, he was the third hurler in the game to notch 300 wins.

Roger Connor, first baseman, several teams, 19th century, elected 1976.

Connor's skills, put to use today, would have made him a contender for all-time home-run honors . . .

Possessed of a great eye and a quick, powerful swing, Connor was the acknowledged four-base hero of the 1880s—when the ball was almost as dead as a stone—walloping 138 lifetime homers, a 19th-century mark that remained on the books until Babe Ruth arrived.

Amos Rusie, pitcher, several teams, 19th century, elected 1977.

A big, hulking hurler, one of the biggest in the pros of his day, Rusie had dazzling speed and one of the great early curves . . . In his 10-year career, won 30 or more games four times in succession, and 20 or more eight straight years . . . Always among the leaders in strikeouts, he may have been the fastest pitcher of his day.

EARLY BLACK STARS IN THE HALL OF FAME

Before Jackie Robinson cracked the color line and became the first black player in the major leagues, there were many great black players who performed in the so-called Negro Leagues throughout the country. Many were good enough to have made the majors if there hadn't been a color line. To acknowledge their greatness, Baseball's Hall of Fame created, in 1972, a special section for those great players in the Negro Leagues. Following are those elected so far.

Buck Leonard, first baseman, Homestead Grays, elected 1972.

One of many stars of the Grays, Leonard as a first sacker was an artist with his glove and would have been a candidate for a Gold Glove award had the

Negro Leagues had that honor in their day . . . His bat helped the Grays to nine straight titles in the Negro National League . . . A constant home-run threat, he won the league batting crown with a lofty .391 in 1948.

Josh Gibson, catcher, Homestead Grays/Pittsburgh Crawfords, elected 1972.

Like many a black player who starred in the Negro Leagues, Josh Gibson surely would have been a star in the majors . . . Gibson, who had great gifts as a backstop, was a sensational hitter whose frequent and mighty home-run blasts awed pitchers and fans alike . . . For years he was the receiver for the legendary Satchel Paige with the Pittsburgh Crawfords.

James Bell, outfielder, several clubs, elected 1974.

Called Cool Papa Bell by his fans, Bell was the Negro Leagues' version of later black base stealers such as Jackie Robinson, Lou Brock, and Rickey Henderson . . . Easily the fastest man ever to play in the Negro Leagues, he delighted his fans and made his foes nervous, whether on the base paths or at the plate, where he was a switch-hitter and sprayed singles and doubles to all fields for 21 seasons.

Judy Johnson, third baseman, Hilldale/
Homestead Grays/Pittsburgh Crawfords,
elected 1975.

Nobody ever teased him for being called Judy . . .
His remarkable fielding at third base took care of
that . . . He cooled off the hot corner with his brilliant
defensive work and few balls ever got past him in
reachable range, and he ranged from the line to anywhere near shortstop . . . Throughout the late 1920s
and into the 1930s he was also a steady .300 hitter.

Oscar Charleston, first baseman/out-
fielder, several clubs, elected 1976.

Whether patrolling center field or doing his nifty
thing at first base, Charleston was supreme with his
glove and throwing arm . . . In the days of loosely
applied contracts with the Negro Leagues, he played
for five or six clubs and was regarded by many black
fans as the best all-around black player of the 1920s,
hitting more than .300 in most of his campaigns . . .
He later managed many black teams.

Martin Dihago, outfielder/infielder/
pitcher, several clubs, elected 1977.

Dihago could play just about any position on the
field—and often did . . . His versatility was famed far
and wide among fans of the Negro Leagues who looked

forward to being surprised at his position when they got to the ball park . . . He also played in three nations: the U.S., Cuba, and Mexico . . . He was so brilliant and consistent that one year in Mexico he had a mound mark of 18–2 with a sensational 0.90 ERA, and also won the league batting title with .387.

John Lloyd, shortstop, several clubs, elected 1977.

Nobody could charge a ball or make the difficult play like John (Pop) Lloyd, who was probably the best fielding shortstop to play in the Negro Leagues . . . He had a magic glove and a great arm . . . At the plate he wasn't noted for the long ball, but he was a spray hitter to all fields, especially with men on base . . . He played for clubs in New York, Chicago, Philadelphia, and smaller cities.

Rube Foster, pitcher, several teams, elected 1981.

Rube Foster was probably the finest pitcher in the Negro Leagues until the legendary Satchel Paige came along . . . Records for black baseball weren't carefully kept, but it was said that he probably had at least 10 seasons when he won 25 games or more in the early part of the century . . . When he managed the Chicago Giants, his club went a phenomenal 123–6 in 1910 . . . Ten years later he was the organizing spirit behind the formal Negro National League.

The Lineup of Legends
Lifetime Records of Hall of Fame Members

FIRST BASEMEN (14)	B-T	HT.	WT.	BIRTHDATE	PLACE OF BIRTH	G	AB	R	H	2B	3B	HR	RBI	PCT
Anson, Cap**	R-R	6-1	227	April 17, 1852	Marshalltown, IA	2253	9084	1712	3081	530	129	92	—	.339
Banks, Ernie*	R-R	6-1	180	Jan. 31, 1931	Dallas, TX	2528	9421	1305	2583	407	90	512	1636	.274
Beckley, Jake*	L-L	5-11	190	Aug. 4, 1867	Hannibal, MO	2373	9476	1601	2930	455	246	87	1575	.309
Bottomley, Jim**	L-L	6-0	180	April 23, 1900	Oglesby, IL	1991	7471	1177	2313	465	151	219	1422	.310
Brouthers, Dan**	L-L	6-2	207	May 8, 1858	Sylvan Lake, NY	1658	6725	1507	2349	446	212	103	—	.349
Chance, Frank**	R-R	6-0	190	Sept. 9, 1877	Fresno, CA	1232	4279	796	1273	195	80	20	596	.297
Connor, Roger**	L-L	6-3	220	July 1, 1857	Waterbury, CT	1987	7807	1607	2535	429	227	138	—	.325
Foxx, Jimmie*	R-R	6-0	200	Oct. 22, 1907	Sudlersville, MD	2317	8134	1751	2646	458	125	534	1921	.325
Gehrig, Lou	L-L	6-0	200	June 19, 1903	New York, NY	2164	8001	1888	2721	535	162	493	1990	.340
Greenberg, Hank*	R-R	6-4	218	Jan. 1, 1911	New York, NY	1394	5193	1051	1628	379	71	331	1276	.313
Kelly, George**	R-R	6-4	190	Sept. 10, 1895	San Francisco, CA	1622	5993	819	1778	337	76	148	1019	.297
Mize, Johnny**	L-R	6-2	215	Jan. 7, 1913	Demorest, GA	1884	6443	1118	2011	367	83	359	1337	.312
Sisler, George*	L-L	5-10½	170	Mar. 24, 1893	Nimisila, OH	2055	8267	1284	2812	425	164	102	1180	.340
Terry, Bill*	L-L	6-1½	200	Oct. 30, 1898	Atlanta, GA	1721	6428	1120	2193	373	112	154	1078	.341

SECOND BASEMEN (8)	B-T	HT.	WT.	BIRTHDATE	PLACE OF BIRTH	G	AB	R	H	2B	3B	HR	RBI	PCT
Collins, Eddie*	L-R	5-9	175	May 2, 1887	Millerton, NY	2825	9949	1819	3312	437	186	47	1307	.333
Evers, Johnny*	L-R	5-9	140	July 21, 1881	Troy, NY	1776	6136	919	1659	216	70	12	538	.270
Frisch, Frank*	Bo-R	5-10	185	Sept. 9, 1897	New York, NY	2311	9112	1532	2880	466	138	105	1242	.316
Gehringer, Charlie*	L-R	5-11½	185	May 11, 1903	Fowlerville, MI	2323	8860	1773	2839	574	146	184	1427	.320
Herman, Billy**	R-R	5-11	185	July 7, 1909	New Albany, IN	1922	7707	1163	2345	486	82	47	839	.304
Hornsby, Rogers*	R-R	5-11	175	April 27, 1896	Winters, TX	2259	8173	1579	2930	541	168	302	1579	.358
Lajoie, Nap*	R-R	6-2	195	Sept. 5, 1875	Woonsocket, RI	2475	9589	1503	3251	650	162	82	1599	.339
Robinson, Jackie*	R-R	6-0	215	Jan. 31, 1919	Cairo, GA	1382	4877	947	1518	273	54	137	734	.311

SHORTSTOPS (12)	B-T	HT.	WT.	BIRTHDATE	PLACE OF BIRTH	G	AB	R	H	2B	3B	HR	RBI	PCT
Appling, Luke*	R-R	5-11	185	April 2, 1907	High Point, NC	2422	8857	1319	2749	440	102	45	1116	.310
Bancroft, Dave**	Bo-R	5-9	140	April 20, 1891	Sioux City, IA	1913	7182	1048	2004	320	77	32	579	.279

SHORTSTOPS (12)	B-T	HT.	WT.	BIRTHDATE	PLACE OF BIRTH	G	AB	R	H	2B	3B	HR	RBI	PCT
Boudreau, Lou*	R-R	5-11	175	July 17, 1917	Harvey, IL	1646	6030	861	1779	385	66	68	789	.295
Cronin, Joe*	R-R	5-11½	180	Oct. 12, 1906	San Francisco, CA	2124	7577	1233	2285	516	118	170	1423	.302
Jackson, Travis*	R-R	5-10½	160	Nov. 2, 1903	Waldo, AR	1656	6086	833	1768	291	86	135	929	.291
Jennings, Hugh**	R-R	5-8½	165	April 2, 1869	Pittston, PA	1264	4840	989	1520	227	88	19	840	.314
Maranville, Rabbit*	R-R	5-5	160	Nov. 11, 1891	Springfield, MA	2670	10078	1255	2605	380	177	28	874	.258
Sewell, Joe**	L-R	5-8	160	Oct. 9, 1898	Titus, AL	1903	7132	1141	2226	436	68	49	1051	.312
Tinker, Joe**	R-R	5-9	175	July 27, 1880	Muscotah, KS	1799	6445	776	1698	262	114	31	783	.263
Wagner, Honus**	R-R	5-11	200	Feb. 24, 1874	Carnegie, PA	2785	10427	1740	3430	651	252	101	1732	.329
Wallace, Bobby**	R-R	5-8	170	Nov. 4, 1874	Pittsburgh, PA	2369	8629	1056	2308	395	149	36	1121	.267
Ward, Monte**	L-R	5-9	165	April 3, 1860	Bellefonte, PA	1810	7579	1403	2151	232	95	26	—	.283

THIRD BASEMEN (5)	B-T	HT.	WT.	BIRTHDATE	PLACE OF BIRTH	G	AB	R	H	2B	3B	HR	RBI	PCT
Baker, Frank**	L-R	5-11½	180	March 13, 1886	Trappe, MD	1575	5985	887	1838	313	103	93	1012	.307
Collins, Jimmy**	R-R	5-8	160	Jan. 16, 1870	Niagara Falls, NY	1718	6792	1057	1999	333	117	62	985	.294
Lindstrom, Fred**	R-R	5-11½	160	Nov. 21, 1905	Chicago, IL	1438	5611	895	1747	301	81	103	779	.311
Mathews, Eddie*	L-R	6-1	200	Oct. 13, 1931	Texarkana, TX	2391	8537	1509	2315	354	72	512	1453	.271
Traynor, Pie**	R-R	6-1	175	Nov. 11, 1899	Framingham, MA	1941	7559	1183	2416	371	164	58	1273	.320

LEFT FIELDERS (14)	B-T	HT.	WT.	BIRTHDATE	PLACE OF BIRTH	G	AB	R	H	2B	3B	HR	RBI	PCT
Burkett, Jesse**	L-L	5-8	155	Dec. 4, 1869	Wheeling, WV	2063	8389	1708	2872	314	185	70	952	.342
Clarke, Fred**	L-R	5-10½	165	Oct. 3, 1872	Winterset, IA	2204	8584	1620	2703	358	219	65	1015	.315
Delahanty, Ed**	R-R	6-1	170	Oct. 30, 1867	Cleveland, OH	1825	7493	1596	2593	508	182	98	1464	.346
Goslin, Goose**	L-R	5-10	170	Oct. 16, 1900	Salem, NJ	2287	8654	1483	2735	500	173	248	1609	.316
Hafey, Chick**	R-R	6-0	185	Feb. 12, 1903	Berkeley, CA	1283	4625	777	1466	341	67	164	833	.317
Kelley, Joe**	R-R	5-11	190	Dec. 9, 1871	Cambridge, MA	1827	6982	1424	2244	353	189	66	1194	.321
Kiner, Ralph*	R-R	6-2	195	Oct. 27, 1922	Santa Rita, NM	1472	5205	971	1451	216	39	369	1015	.279
Manush, Heinie**	L-L	6-1½	190	July 20, 1901	Tuscumbia, AL	2009	7653	1287	2524	491	160	110	1173	.330
Medwick, Joe*	R-R	5-10	185	Nov. 24, 1911	Carteret, NJ	1984	7635	1198	2471	540	113	205	1383	.324
Musial, Stan*	L-L	6-0	180	Nov. 21, 1920	Donora, PA	3026	10972	1949	3630	725	177	475	1951	.331
O'Rourke, Jim**	R-R	5-8	185	Aug. 24, 1852	East Bridgeport, CT	1750	7365	1425	2314	385	139	49	—	.314
Simmons, Al*	R-R	6-0	210	May 22, 1903	Milwaukee, WI	2215	8761	1507	2927	539	149	307	1827	.334
Wheat, Zack**	L-R	5-10	180	May 23, 1888	Hamilton, MO	2406	9106	1289	2884	476	172	132	1265	.317
Williams, Ted*	L-R	6-4	198	Aug. 30, 1918	San Diego, CA	2292	7706	1798	2654	525	71	521	1839	.344

CENTER FIELDERS (15)

Name	B-T	HT.	WT.	BIRTHDATE	PLACE OF BIRTH	G	AB	R	H	2B	3B	HR	RBI	PCT
Averill, Earl**	L-R	5-9½	170	May 21, 1902	Snohomish, WA	1669	6358	1224	2020	401	128	238	1165	.318
Carey, Max**	Bo-R	6-0	166	Jan. 11, 1890	Terre Haute, IN	2466	9363	1545	2665	419	159	69	797	.285
Cobb, Ty*	L-R	6-1	175	Dec. 18, 1886	Narrows, GA	3034	11437	2245	4192	724	297	118	1954	.367
Combs, Earle**	L-R	6-0	165	May 14, 1899	Pebworth, KY	1455	5748	1186	1866	309	154	58	629	.325
Cuyler, Kiki**	R-R	5-10½	180	Aug. 30, 1899	Harrisville, MI	1879	7161	1305	2299	394	158	157	1065	.321
DiMaggio, Joe*	R-R	6-1	195	Nov. 25, 1914	Martinez, CA	1736	6821	1390	2214	389	131	361	1537	.325
Duffy, Hugh**	R-R	5-7	168	Nov. 26, 1866	River Point, RI	1722	6999	1545	2307	310	117	103	1299	.330
Hamilton, Billy**	L-L	5-6	165	Feb. 16, 1866	Newark, NJ	1578	6262	1690	2157	225	94	37	736	.344
Mantle, Mickey*	Bo-R	6-0	200	Oct. 20, 1931	Spavinaw, OK	2401	8102	1677	2415	344	72	536	1509	.298
Mays, Willie*	R-R	5-11	187	May 6, 1931	Westfield, AL	2992	10881	2062	3283	523	140	660	1903	.302
Roush, Edd**	L-L	5-11	175	May 8, 1893	Oakland City, IN	1967	7363	1099	2376	339	183	67	981	.323
Snider, Duke*	L-R	6-0	200	Sept. 19, 1926	Los Angeles, CA	2143	7161	1259	2116	358	85	407	1333	.295
Speaker, Tris*	L-L	5-11½	193	April 4, 1888	Hubbard, TX	2789	10208	1881	3515	793	224	115	1559	.344
Waner, Lloyd**	L-R	5-9	145	March 16, 1906	Harrah, OK	1993	7772	1201	2459	281	118	28	598	.316
Wilson, Hack*	R-R	5-6	195	April 26, 1900	Ellwood City, PA	1348	4760	884	1461	266	67	244	1062	.307

RIGHT FIELDERS (18)

Name	B-T	HT.	WT.	BIRTHDATE	PLACE OF BIRTH	G	AB	R	H	2B	3B	HR	RBI	PCT
Aaron, Henry*	R-R	6-0	180	Feb. 5, 1934	Mobile, AL	3298	12364	2174	3771	624	98	755	2297	.305
Clemente, Roberto*	R-R	5-11	182	Aug. 18, 1934	Carolina, PR	2433	9454	1416	3000	440	166	240	1305	.317
Crawford, Sam**	L-L	5-11	190	April 18, 1880	Wahoo, NB	2505	9579	1392	2964	455	312	95	1525	.309
Flick, Elmer**	L-R	5-9	168	Jan. 11, 1876	Bedford, OH	1480	5597	948	1764	268	170	46	756	.315
Heilmann, Harry*	R-R	6-1	200	Aug. 3, 1894	San Francisco, CA	2146	7787	1291	2660	542	151	183	1549	.342
Hooper, Harry**	L-R	5-10	165	Aug. 24, 1887	Bell Station, CA	2308	8784	1429	2466	389	160	75	813	.281
Kaline, Al*	R-R	6-2	184	Dec. 19, 1934	Baltimore, MD	2834	10116	1622	3007	498	75	399	1583	.297
Keeler, Willie*	L-L	5-4½	140	March 13, 1872	Brooklyn, NY	2124	8564	1720	2955	234	155	32	810	.345
Kelly, King**	R-R	5-11	180	Dec. 31, 1857	Troy, NY	1434	5922	1359	1853	351	109	65	—	.313
Klein, Chuck**	L-R	6-0	185	Oct. 7, 1904	Indianapolis, IN	1753	6486	1168	2076	398	74	300	1201	.320
McCarthy, Tommy**	R-R	5-6	145	July 24, 1864	Boston, MA	1258	5055	1050	1485	194	58	43	—	.294
Ott, Mel*	L-R	5-9	165	March 2, 1909	Gretna, LA	2730	9456	1859	2876	488	72	511	1860	.304
Rice, Sam**	L-R	5-9	150	Feb. 20, 1890	Morroco, IN	2404	9269	1515	2987	497	184	34	1077	.322
Robinson, Frank*	R-R	6-1	183	Aug. 31, 1935	Beaumont, TX	2808	10006	1829	2943	528	72	586	1812	.294
Ruth, Babe*	L-L	6-2	215	Feb. 6, 1895	Baltimore, MD	2503	8399	2174	2873	506	136	714	2204	.342
Thompson, Sam**	L-L	6-2	207	March 5, 1860	Danville, IN	1405	6004	1259	2016	326	146	128	1299	.336
Waner, Paul*	L-L	5-8	148	April 16, 1903	Harrah, OK	2549	9459	1626	3152	603	190	112	1309	.333
Youngs, Ross**	L-R	5-8	162	April 10, 1897	Shiner, TX	1211	4627	812	1491	236	93	42	596	.322

CATCHERS (8)	B-T	HT.	WT.	BIRTHDATE	PLACE OF BIRTH	G	AB	R	H	2B	3B	HR	RBI	PCT
Berra, Yogi*	L-R	5-7½	190	May 12, 1925	St. Louis, MO	2120	7555	1175	2150	321	49	358	1430	.285
Bresnahan, Roger**	R-R	5-8	180	June 11, 1879	Toledo, OH	1410	4480	684	1251	222	72	26	531	.279
Campanella, Roy*	R-R	5-9½	190	Nov. 19, 1921	Philadelphia, PA	1215	4205	627	1161	178	18	242	856	.276
Cochrane, Mickey*	L-R	5-10½	180	April 6, 1903	Bridgewater, MA	1482	5169	1041	1652	333	64	119	832	.320
Dickey, Bill*	L-R	6-1½	185	June 6, 1907	Bastrop, LA	1789	6300	930	1969	343	72	202	1209	.313
Ewing, Buck**	R-R	5-10	188	Oct. 17, 1859	Hoaglands, OH	1281	5348	1118	1663	237	179	66	—	.311
Hartnett, Gabby*	R-R	6-2	190	Dec. 20, 1900	Woonsocket, RI	1990	6432	867	1912	396	64	236	1179	.297
Schalk, Ray**	R-R	5-9	154	Aug. 12, 1892	Harvel, IL	1760	5306	579	1345	199	48	12	596	.253

PITCHERS (42)	B-T	HT.	WT.	BIRTHDATE	PLACE OF BIRTH	G	IP	SHO	W	L	PCT	H	SO	BB	ERA
Alexander, Grover*	R-R	6-1	185	Feb. 26, 1887	Elba, NB	696	5189	90	373	208	.642	4868	2198	951	2.56
Bender, Chief**	R-R	6-2	185	May 5, 1884	Brainerd, MN	459	3026	41	212	128	.624	2653	1720	705	2.46
Brown, Mordecai**	Bo-R	5-10	175	Oct. 19, 1876	Nyesville, IN	481	3168	55	239	130	.631	2707	1381	674	2.03
Chesbro, Jack**	R-R	5-9	180	June 5, 1874	North Adams, MA	392	2886	35	198	127	.609	2602	1276	674	2.68
Clarkson, John**	R-R	5-10	160	July 1, 1861	Cambridge, MA	517	4514	37	327	176	.650	4384	2013	1192	—
Coveleski, Stan**	R-R	5-9½	175	July 13, 1889	Shamokin, PA	450	3083	38	216	142	.603	3055	981	802	2.87
Dean, Dizzy*	R-R	6-3	185	Jan. 16, 1911	Lucas, AR	317	1966	27	150	83	.644	1921	1155	458	3.04
Faber, Red**	Bo-R	6-0	190	Sept. 6, 1888	Cascade, IA	669	4087	29	254	212	.545	4104	1471	1213	3.15
Feller, Bob**	R-R	6-0	185	Nov. 3, 1918	Van Meter, IA	570	3828	46	266	162	.621	3271	2581	1764	3.25
Ford, Whitey*	L-L	5-10	180	Oct. 21, 1928	New York, NY	498	3171	45	236	106	.690	2766	1956	1086	2.74
Galvin, Pud**	R-R	5-8	190	Dec. 25, 1855	St. Louis, MO	675	5959	57	361	309	.539	6334	1786	744	—
Gibson, Bob*	R-R	6-1	193	Nov. 9, 1935	Omaha, NB	528	3885	56	251	174	.591	3279	3117	1336	2.91
Gomez, Lefty**	L-L	6-2	175	Nov. 26, 1908	Rodeo, CA	368	2503	28	189	102	.649	2290	1468	1095	3.34
Grimes, Burleigh**	R-R	5-10	185	Aug. 18, 1893	Clear Lake, WI	615	4178	35	270	212	.560	4406	1512	1295	3.52
Grove, Lefty*	L-L	6-3	190	March 6, 1900	Lonaconing, MD	616	3940	35	300	141	.680	3849	2266	1187	3.06
Haines, Jess**	R-R	6-0	190	July 22, 1893	Clayton, OH	555	3207	23	210	158	.571	3460	981	871	3.64
Hoyt, Waite**	R-R	5-11	183	Sept. 9, 1899	Brooklyn, NY	674	3762	26	237	182	.566	4037	1206	1003	3.59
Hubbell, Carl*	R-L	6-2	172	June 22, 1903	Carthage, MO	535	3591	36	253	154	.622	3461	1677	725	2.98
Johnson, Walter*	R-R	6-1	200	Nov. 6, 1887	Humboldt, KS	802	5924	113	416	279	.599	4920	3508	1353	2.17
Joss, Addie**	R-R	6-3	185	April 12, 1880	Juneau, WI	286	2333	45	160	97	.623	1889	915	357	—
Keefe, Tim**	R-R	5-10½	185	Jan. 1, 1857	Cambridge, MA	599	5050	40	344	225	.605	4452	2542	1225	—
Koufax, Sandy*	R-L	6-2	202	Dec. 30, 1935	Brooklyn, NY	397	2325	40	165	87	.655	1754	2396	817	2.76
Lemon, Bob*	L-R	6-0	180	Sept. 22, 1920	San Bernardino, CA	460	2849	31	207	128	.618	2559	1277	1251	3.23
Lyons, Ted*	Bo-R	6-0	185	Dec. 28, 1900	Lake Charles, LA	594	4162	27	260	230	.531	4489	1073	1121	3.67

PITCHERS (42)	B-T	HT.	WT.	BIRTHDATE	PLACE OF BIRTH	G	IP	SHO	W	L	PCT	H	SO	BB	ERA
Marquard, Rube**	Bo-L	6-3½	175	Oct. 9, 1889	Cleveland, OH	536	3307	30	201	177	.532	3233	1593	858	3.08
Mathewson, Christy*	R-R	6-1½	195	Aug. 12, 1880	Factoryville, PA	635	4781	83	373	188	.665	4203	2505	837	2.13
McGinnity, Joe**	R-R	5-11	206	March 19, 1871	Rock Island, IL	467	3455	32	247	145	.630	3236	1058	803	2.66
Nichols, Kid**	R-R	5-10½	175	Sept. 14, 1869	Madison, WI	582	5067	48	360	202	.641	4854	1866	1245	2.95
Pennock, Herb*	Bo-L	6-0	165	Feb. 10, 1894	Kennett Square, PA	617	3558	35	240	162	.597	3900	1227	916	3.55
Plank, Eddie**	L-L	5-11½	175	Aug. 31, 1875	Gettysburg, PA	623	4503	69	326	192	.629	3898	2257	1042	2.34
Radbourne, Old Hoss**	R-R	5-9	168	Dec. 11, 1854	Rochester, NY	517	4543	35	308	191	.617	4500	1746	856	—
Rixey, Eppa**	R-L	6-5½	210	May 3, 1891	Culpeper, VA	692	4494	39	266	251	.515	4633	1350	1082	3.15
Roberts, Robin*	Bo-R	6-1	200	Sept. 30, 1926	Springfield, IL	676	4689	45	286	245	.539	4582	2357	902	3.40
Ruffing, Red*	R-R	6-1½	215	May 3, 1905	Granville, IL	624	4342	46	273	225	.548	4294	1987	1541	3.80
Rusie, Amos**	R-R	6-1	200	May 30, 1871	Mooresville, IN	462	3772	31	245	174	.585	3384	1934	1704	—
Spahn, Warren*	L-L	6-0	185	April 23, 1921	Buffalo, NY	750	5246	63	363	245	.597	4830	2583	1434	3.08
Vance, Dazzy**	R-R	6-2	200	March 4, 1891	Orient, IA	442	2967	31	197	140	.585	2809	2045	840	3.24
Waddell, Rube**	R-L	6-1½	196	Oct. 13, 1876	Bradford, PA	407	2958	50	191	142	.574	2480	2310	771	2.16
Walsh, Ed**	R-R	6-1	193	May 14, 1881	Plains, PA	431	2968	58	195	126	.607	2335	1731	620	1.82
Welch, Mickey**	R-R	5-8	160	July 4, 1859	Brooklyn, NY	565	4566	41	308	209	.596	4648	1841	1305	—
Wynn, Early*	Bo-R	6-0	220	Jan. 6, 1920	Hartford, AL	691	4566	49	300	244	.551	4291	2334	1775	3.54
Young, Cy*	R-R	6-2	210	March 29, 1867	Gilmore, OH	906	7377	77	511	313	.620	7078	2819	1209	2.63

FROM NEGRO LEAGUES (10)	BIRTHDATE	PLACE OF BIRTH
Bell, Cool Papa***	May 17, 1903	Starkville, MS
Charleston, Oscar***	Oct. 14, 1896	Indianapolis, IN
Dihigo, Martin***	May 25, 1906	Matanzas, Cuba
Foster, Rube**	Sept. 17, 1879	Calvert, TX
Gibson, Josh***	Dec. 21, 1911	Buena Vista, GA
Irvin, Monte***	Feb. 25, 1919	Columbia, AL
Johnson, Judy***	Oct. 26, 1899	Snow Hill, MD
Leonard, Buck***	Sept. 8, 1907	Rocky Mount, NC
Lloyd, John***	April 25, 1884	Gainesville, FL
Paige, Satchel***	July 7, 1906	Mobile, AL

*Elected by Baseball Writers Association of America
**Elected by Hall of Fame Committee on Baseball Veterans
***Elected by Hall of Fame Committee on Negro Baseball Leagues

NOTE: RBI's were not kept officially until 1920.

ERA's became an official statistic in 1912 (NL) and 1913 (AL).